Into the Classroom

Thomas Hatch

with

Melissa Eiler White

Jason Raley

Kimberlee Austin

Sarah Capitelli

Deborah Faigenbaum

Foreword by Lee S. Shulman

Into the Classroom

Developing the Scholarship of Teaching and Learning

JOSSEY-BASS
A Wiley Imprint
www.josseybass.com

Published by Jossey-Bass
A Wiley Imprint
989 Market Street, San Francisco, CA 94103-1741   www.josseybass.com

Jossey-Bass books and products are available through most bookstores. To contact Jossey-Bass directly call our Customer Care Department within the U.S. at 800-956-7739, outside the U.S. at 317-572-3986, or fax 317-572-4002.

Jossey-Bass also publishes its books in a variety of electronic formats. Some content that appears in print may not be available in electronic books.

Library of Congress Cataloging-in-Publication Data

Hatch, Thomas.
  Into the classroom : developing the scholarship of teaching and learning / Thomas Hatch, with Melissa Eiler White ... [et al.].— 1st ed.
    p. cm. — (Jossey-Bass education series)
  Includes bibliographical references and index.
  ISBN-13: 978-0-7879-8108-2 (alk. paper)
  ISBN-10: 0-7879-8108-7 (alk. paper)
  1. Teaching—United States.   2. Communication in learning and scholarship—United States.   3. Teachers—Professional relationships—United States.   I. Title.   II. Series.
  LB1027.H348 2005
  371.102—dc22

                                                                                2005012619

Printed in the United States of America
FIRST EDITION
HB Printing   10 9 8 7 6 5 4 3 2 1

Contents

Foreword

When one hears the phrase "the scholarship of teaching and learning," the first impulse is to imagine a K–12 classroom in which faculty members and graduate students from the university are sitting around its perimeter, taking extensive notes on lined yellow pads, making videos of the interactions, and conducting interviews with the participants. Scholarship is an experience that teachers undergo; it is not one they undertake. They are the objects of scholarship, not its initiators. They are thanked in forewords or acknowledged in footnotes, not recognized as authors and designers of the studies. Indeed, as Judy Shulman observed in an article aptly titled "Now You See Them, Now You Don't: Anonymity Versus Visibility in the Study of Teaching," for years our primary efforts were directed at keeping the identities of teachers confidential rather than at ensuring that they received full and public credit for their contributions to research. This book is part of the counterrevolution with respect to those expectations. In this volume, "the scholarship of teaching and learning" refers to what teachers themselves *do*, from design and execution to dissemination and publication.

During my career, I have worked extensively in both medical education and in the education of teachers. This twin focus has given me the opportunity to explore a variety of features shared by the two fields—and by other professional areas, as well. It has also brought into sharp focus one very consequential difference between them: while medicine has developed a whole host of ways to document and share practice, and thus to improve it, the work of teachers (as I have written elsewhere) too often disappears like dry ice at room temperature. It is this problem that Tom Hatch takes on in this wonderful new volume.

My own sense of the problem began, really, when I entered the professoriate.

Life at the University of Chicago, where I was both an undergraduate and graduate student, was rich with opportunities for exchange with colleagues. Faculty members and students gathered together on a daily basis to exchange ideas and gossip, tough criticisms and good yarns. It was one of the things that made life at Chicago so rich and rewarding.

But when I moved on to my first faculty position as a newly-minted, full-fledged Ph.D., I discovered a much different reality. As researchers, my colleagues and I had energetic interactions, both within the institution and across institutional boundaries. The teaching life, however, was a private experience, shared with students but almost never with faculty colleagues. Working with students was wonderful. But when it came to colleagues, the classroom turned out to be a lonely place, an experience of pedagogical solitude. And this, alas, has been true, across all levels of education, from the elementary grades to graduate school.

However, as Hatch documents in the pages that follow, this unhappy situation has begun to change. Teaching and learning are now, increasingly, a focus for conversation among teachers at all levels, and the subject of lively intellectual exchange. New models for capturing what experienced teachers know and do are emerging, and the prospect of building (and building on) a rich history of practice is beginning to be a reality. There are certainly many forces and factors contributing to these developments, but one of the most important is the scholarship of teaching and learning.

As many readers will know, the scholarship of teaching and learning is a major theme of The Carnegie Foundation, one that has been central to our work for some time and is likely to be one of our most important legacies. The Carnegie Academy for the Scholarship of Teaching and Learning (which we call CASTL) has been our special program in this area, but the habits, values, and commitments of such work run through all of Carnegie's projects, whether on K–12, undergraduate, or graduate and professional education. The scholarship of teaching and learning invites faculty at all these levels to view teaching as serious, intellectual work, ask good questions about their students' learning, seek evidence in their classrooms that can be used to improve practice, and make this work public so that others can critique it, build on it, and contribute to the wider teaching commons. In many fields, we now expect practice to become increasingly "evidence-based." But in the scholarship of teaching and learning, we also insist that a "culture of evidence" be built around the scholarship conducted by practitioners themselves, in addition to devoting careful attention to the scholarship of external scholars and scientists.

In *Into the Classroom*, Hatch draws especially on the Foundation's work with K–12 teachers who have participated as fellows in the Carnegie Academy for the Scholarship of Teaching and Learning. As one of the leaders of that work while he was a senior scholar here at the Foundation (in 2004 he moved to his present position at Teachers College), Hatch had the incredible opportunity to observe and support the work of these teachers, up close and over time. Tracing their efforts and experiences through a series of case studies, he uncovers a powerful cascade of activity and impact. It turns out that documenting and reflecting on practice is not only a powerful prompt for improvement by individual teachers; it is a context for building scholarly community about teaching and learning. Instilling the disposition to engage in such scholarly work on one's own practice holds the potential for impact on colleagues, institutions, and policy.

It is interesting to contrast this approach to improvement with one of the earliest accomplishments from The Carnegie Foundation's historical legacy. Beginning with the Flexner Report in the period of 1908 to 1910, the Foundation pioneered the external investigation, review, and evaluation of the work of education. Employing teams of outside experts, the Foundation conducted incisive studies of the quality of education in undergraduate programs and in the professions, including teacher education and work in K–12 classrooms. This work prefigured the current climate of account-ability and external oversight of the work of our educational institu-tions. However, in later years, and increasingly today, the Foundation also began to communicate a very different message: improvement was not achieved simply by responding to external evaluations of quality. Rather—and this is a central message of the scholarship of teaching and learning—it is the professional responsibility of edu-cators to engage continuously in their own efforts to study the qual-ity of their work, its fidelity to their missions, and its impact on students intellectually, practically, and morally.

It is the promise of this approach that Hatch's work captures so thoughtfully and so vividly. As he points out, there is of course much work yet to be done, and many challenges to grapple with in turning teaching from "a private practice to a learning profession." But I am hard-pressed to imagine work more appropriate to the Foundation's mission as articulated by Andrew Carnegie 100 years ago this year: "to do and perform all things necessary to encourage, uphold, and dignify the profession of the teacher." Few things can bring greater dignity to teaching at all levels than the expectation that teachers themselves hold the ability and responsibility for learning from their own practice and systemically improving it. I hope that readers will find this volume and its message as hearten-ing as I do.

—Lee S. Shulman
Stanford, California
June 2005

Preface

Making Teaching Public

> What do we mean when we call something "scholarship"? Certainly, all acts of intelligence are not scholarship. An act of intelligence or of artistic creation becomes scholarship when it possesses at least three attributes: it becomes public; it becomes an object of critical review and evaluation by members of one's community; and members of one's community begin to use, build upon, and develop those acts of mind and creation.
>
> —*Lee S. Shulman*, Taking Learning Seriously

The American educational system is a "public" system, yet most of what goes on in schools remains unseen. Learning happens behind closed doors, inside fences, and on campuses cut off from the rest of the community. With few sustained opportunities to go into the classrooms of their peers or to discuss their work together, teachers cannot learn from or build on the accomplishments of their peers. One teacher may develop an exemplary fifth grade curriculum in American History and another may learn how to help high school students gain a robust understanding of key concepts in biology or algebra, but when they leave the classroom they cannot leave their expertise for others. They may take what they have learned to a new school or another line of work, but the new teachers who come to occupy the same rooms and teach the same courses have to learn the same lessons all over again.

Similarly, parents, community members, and policymakers have neither the time nor the means to go into many classrooms. Educators, parents, and the general public have to rely on secondary sources such as test scores and grade reports rather than direct observation in order to judge the quality of students' educational experiences. Even students have few opportunities to see how their work compares to the work of their peers in classrooms across town and around the country. As a consequence, although the American educational system is designed to provide considerable local control, most people lack the means to decide for themselves whether the schools in their community meet their expectations.

It would be unthinkable for doctors or scientists to have only limited access to the work or discoveries of their colleagues. Without ways for these professionals to document what they do and to share their results with their peers for discussion, verification, and further investigation, the examination and advancement of medical and scientific knowledge would be seriously constrained. Fortunately, doctors and scientists work in professions in which they can make their own insights and discoveries public. Teachers, unfortunately, do not. With the status quo in teaching and learning far from sufficient and the demands for improvements increasing, we can no longer afford the knowledge drain that exists because there are few systematic and widespread means for teachers to develop and share their expertise with others.

This book grows out of one initiative designed to support a movement to make teaching public: The Carnegie Academy for the Scholarship of Teaching and Learning (CASTL). The *scholarship of teaching* refers to efforts by faculty members at all levels to make teaching public so that others can critique it and build upon it. CASTL was designed by members of the Carnegie Foundation for the Advancement of Teaching to support the development of the scholarship of teaching and to bring to teaching the recognition and rewards that benefit scholars in so many other disciplines.

The Carnegie Academy for the Scholarship of Teaching and Learning

The Carnegie Academy for the Scholarship of Teaching and Learning (CASTL) has supported the development of the scholarship of teaching through the establishment of several fellowship programs for faculty in both higher education and K–12. The idea for the CASTL program originated in a "peer review" project in higher education that Pat Hutchings and Lee Shulman worked on before they joined the Carnegie Foundation. Since the launch of the first cohort of fifteen higher education scholars in 1998 and the first cohort of nineteen K–12 teachers and teacher educators in 1999, CASTL has provided one- or two-year fellowships in which faculty investigate a key issue in their teaching in a project of their own design. During the fellowships, faculty met with other members of their cohort and, often, other returning CASTL scholars for a summer "residency" at the Carnegie Foundation for the Advancement of Teaching that ranged from a weekend to a week or more. During the year, scholars remained connected through a virtual network and met periodically to share their developing work with one another and with outside audiences.

By the end of 2004, the CASTL program had supported the work of over one hundred fifty faculty in higher education and over sixty faculty members from K–12 or teacher education. Currently, CASTL provides similar fellowship opportunities, but they are usually focused around a particular issue or area, such as the liberal arts or teacher education.

My own involvement in CASTL began with my participation in the development of the program in higher education and then my work as codirector, with Ann Lieberman, of the program for elementary, secondary, and teacher educators. The chapters reflect as well some of my experiences as a founder of the Carnegie Knowledge Media Lab (KML), which I codirected with Toru Iiyoshi. The KML was launched, in Lee Shulman's words, to provide in virtual fashion all the resources of the traditional university—the laboratory, library, and museum—for the members of the CASTL programs and others pursuing the scholarship of teaching (see the KML website for more information: www.carnegiefoundation.org/KML/index.htm).

The KML has gone on to create a number of websites that document the work of a wide range of teachers (see Chapter Five) and to develop a variety of tools and resources to enable others to create their own web-based representations of teaching.

The Design of the Book

In this book, I argue that by making teaching public—making it possible for many people to see the nature and quality of the teaching that goes on inside schools—we can create unprecedented opportunities for teachers to learn from one another and for policymakers and the general public to participate constructively in supporting and improving schools. To that end, I examine the experiences of a number of teachers who make their work public. In the process, I chronicle many of the assumptions and issues that must be confronted in order to turn teaching into a learning profession in which teachers can develop their expertise and share it with others.

This book is designed for a wide audience of practitioners and researchers. In particular, it aims to inform those who design, lead, and study professional development and teacher preparation initiatives. Although the chapters focus particularly on the role of teachers' own inquiries in advancing learning, the challenges and issues are common to many forms of professional development. In addition, the book is intended to help administrators, policymakers, and other educational decision makers to envision and enact new ways to build up and build on the vast expertise in teaching and learning that exists in the field.

The chapters in this book chronicle the work of a small group of the K–12 teachers who participated in the first or second cohort of the CASTL program. In the process, it traces the evolution of some of the key issues of the scholarship of teaching over the course of CASTL's first six years. Following a brief overview of the development of the scholarship of teaching and learning, Chapter One presents the rationale for pursuing the scholarship of teaching and for making teaching public, and describes some of the key issues and assumptions that confront those who seek to do so. Chapter Two reports on the experiences of three members of the first cohort of K–12 and teacher education scholars and documents what these teachers must do to deal with the absence of the social and intellectual infrastructure that supports scholarship in other fields. Chapters Three and Four move from a focus on the challenges of making teaching public to examining what members of the second cohort of K–12 scholars learned as they made their teaching public and the ways in which their inquiries contributed to the work of their peers and the profession as a whole. Chapter Five looks at some recent efforts to use technology to make teaching public and to build on teachers' expertise in teacher preparation and professional development. Chapter Six looks ahead to consider some of the key developments needed to make teaching public on a wider scale—including the development of a new infrastructure for teaching and learning.

Several basic ideas run throughout these chapters. First, to make teaching public, faculty at all levels need new means for documenting and representing what they do in the classroom; current research methods and conventional genres of scholarship can be useful, but they are not sufficient for capturing the complexity of teaching or conveying the expertise needed to do it effectively in many different contexts and situations. Second, progress in the scholarship of teaching and in making teaching public will also depend on establishing new forums for the presentation, publication, and review of teachers' work. Third, simply providing access to teachers' work is not the same thing as making it accessible; we also have to develop an audience for teachers' work and build the collective capacity to interpret and assess what goes in the classroom.

Perhaps most important, all the chapters in this book confront a basic contradiction in some of the most prominent strategies for improving schools and student performance in the United States. On the one hand, many of the policies and initiatives designed to improve student performance invest heavily in directing teachers' activities, monitoring their performance, and controlling the "quality" of the outcomes of their work. Such strategies are based on a view of teachers as nonprofessionals, ill-trained and unprepared, incapable of making decisions in the best interests of the students and communities they serve. On the other hand, many policies and initiatives that aim to ensure that all students have access to "high-quality" teaching revolve around efforts to develop the preparation and professional development programs that can attract and sustain the best and brightest in careers in education. Such efforts are based on a view of teachers as professionals who can learn from their experiences and make the choices and exercise the judgment that will facilitate the growth and development of their students.

Of course, resolving this contradiction is not entirely an either/or proposition. We can have some high and common standards, strong supports for effective teaching, and means of identifying, assisting, or ultimately removing ineffective teachers, but the work described in this book suggests that we cannot simultaneously treat teachers as if they have to be tightly controlled and expect many of them to develop the professional responsibility for learning from their experiences and sharing their experiences with others that lies at the heart of the scholarship of teaching.

Overview

Scholarship of Teaching and Learning

The term *scholarship of teaching* encompasses a variety of different connotations for both *scholarship* and *teaching*. Scholarship can be seen as a noble enterprise or an arcane pursuit that relies on anachronistic methods. Teaching can be viewed as a vigorous intellectual endeavor or a routine engagement—more of an obligation to impart information than an opportunity to learn. At their worst, these terms can conjure up images of the scholarship of teaching as abstract, academic efforts to examine uninteresting phenomena, irrelevant for the advancement of the disciplines. But at their best, these terms together suggest efforts to articulate and examine issues key to the disciplines, development, and education that breathe new life into both scholarship and teaching.

Scholarship in Historical Perspective

To reflect the best of both worlds, the scholarship of teaching demands both a certain respect for scholarship and teaching and a healthy skepticism about the effectiveness of the methods and forms of doing both. In particular, the scholarship of teaching requires a fundamental rethinking of the conventional view of scholarship. Today when people think of scholarship they often focus on the products of scholarship—usually texts—with certain properties. The precise properties may vary from discipline to discipline, but in the United States we tend to think of scholarship as the texts that are the products of inquiries and investigations of academics and other researchers. But over the ages, scholarship was not simply defined by the characteristics of certain products. To understand the history of scholarship, it is necessary to understand who scholars were and what kinds of activities they were involved in, not just what kinds of products they produced. For example, in some ancient societies being a scholar meant that one was a scribe who was involved in activities such as the production of manuscripts, compositions, and religious chants (Huber, 1993). In many ancient civilizations, priests, orators, and government officials who were involved in public and civic activities were viewed as scholars. In the middle ages, the word *scholar* first appeared and was typically used to refer to university students who were involved in preparations for studying ancient texts. At the end of the nineteenth century in the United States, the term *scholar* was used to refer primarily to college professors, but the scholarly activities of those professors were viewed relatively broadly and encompassed their efforts to prepare students for work and civil service and to discover knowledge relevant to practice. It was only with the advent of the development of the research university in the twentieth century that scholarship has come to be associated almost exclusively with the production of research in certain forms specified by the disciplines (Huber, 1993).

Along with the increasing connection between research and scholarship, peer review—in which one or more experts evaluate the work produced by other members of their field—has become a "gold standard" as a means of assessing scholarship. Despite persistent questions about the value of peer review, formal processes of peer review in hiring and evaluation, publication, and funding decisions are seen as the central forums for discussing work, for developing criteria and standards, and for determining the value and quality of ideas and scholarship. But such formal means of peer review rely on many more informal opportunities for scholars to examine one another's work. In fact, in many ways, the formal mechanisms for the peer review of scholarship in a wide range of disciplines have grown out of the informal processes of information- and idea-sharing that have always been a key aspect of the generation and exchange of knowledge:

In the broadest sense of the term, *peer review* can be said to have existed ever since people began to communicate what they thought was new knowledge. That is because peer review (whether it occurs before or after publication) is an essential and integral process of consensus building and is inherent and necessary to the growth of scientific knowledge. (Kronick, 1990, p. 1321)

Thus, while some of the formal mechanisms of peer review were first used for the publications of the royal scientific societies in England in the eighteenth century, those societies first fostered the development of communities of scholars in which the informal review and exchange of ideas could take place on a regular basis. In these communities, participants had the opportunity to develop methods, language, and criteria of quality especially suited to the demands of their growing disciplines. As this brief history suggests, scholarship—and the scholarship of teaching—does not have to be defined simply by what properties a product has or by whether or not it passes through a formal process of review; scholarship can be seen as encompassing the informal and formal activities in which individuals and groups engage in making their ideas public and advancing knowledge.

The Roots of the "Scholarship of Teaching"

In many ways, the publications of *Scholarship Reconsidered* (Boyer, 1990) and *Scholarship Assessed* (Glassick, Huber, & Maeroff, 1997)—growing out of the work of Ernest Boyer, Gene Rice, Mary Huber, and their colleagues at the Carnegie Foundation for the Advancement of Teaching—launched the use of the term *scholarship of teaching* in discussions in higher education. As a result, many assume that the work on the scholarship of teaching of Lee Shulman—who succeeded Boyer as president of the Carnegie Foundation—is rooted in those same publications. However, Shulman comes to the scholarship of teaching from an entirely different perspective: from that of his predecessors at the Foundation. In many ways, the two approaches

are complementary. At the same time, the differences in perspective reflect somewhat different uses of the term *scholarship of teaching* and lead them to different starting points when seeking to
support improvements in teaching.

These differences emerge in the areas of emphasis of each approach. In *Scholarship Reconsidered* and *Scholarship Assessed* the emphasis is on improving the quality of higher education, on scholarship
rather than teaching, and on expanding the categories of activities
that scholarship encompasses. From this perspective, a key problem
in efforts to improve higher education is a reward system that has
come to value the production and publication of research to the virtual exclusion of numerous other important activities in which faculty should be—and traditionally have been—engaged:

"Today, on campuses, the reward system does not match the full
range of academic functions and professors are often caught between competing obligations. In response, there is a lively and
growing discussion about how faculty should, in fact, spend their
time" (Boyer, 1990, p. 1).

Thus *Scholarship Reconsidered* challenged the narrow equation
of scholarship with research—which the authors termed the *scholarship of discovery*. They argued that the term *scholarship* should be
broadened to apply not only to teaching, but also to application and
integration. *Scholarship Assessed* continued this challenge by propos-
ing standards by which to judge scholarly performance in each of
these areas.

This view, which some have called the "Boyer model," grows out
of a long history of work on higher education and efforts to improve
it. Although Boyer—former chancellor of the State University of
New York and commissioner of education in the early seventies—
and his colleagues at the Carnegie Foundation had focused some attention on elementary and secondary education, their work on
scholarship focused primarily on higher education. Furthermore,
consistent with the origins and much of the work of the Carnegie
Foundation since its founding—which began by creating pensions

for professors (eventually leading to the creation of TIAA-CREF, now the largest retirement fund for educators at all levels)—this effort sought to improve the quality of higher education by focusing on incentives and rewards and by supporting changes in the policies governing them.

For Shulman, however, a key problem in efforts to improve teaching has been an impoverished understanding of the knowledge and skills needed to teach. In response, his emphasis has been on expanding the knowledge base for teaching, not necessarily expanding the categories of scholarship. A psychologist by training, Shulman has developed these views in a career studying teaching (often, though not exclusively, teachers in secondary schools), and he has done so by examining different forms of research on teaching and illuminating the ways in which that research shapes views of what teachers need to know and be able to do. As he put it in "Paradigms and Research Programs in the Study of Teaching: A Contemporary Perspective": Knowledge does not grow naturally or inexorably. It is produced through the inquiries of scholars—empiricists, theorists, practitioners—and is, therefore, a function of the kinds of questions asked, problems posed, and issues framed by those who do research. The framing of a research question, like that of an attorney in a court of law, limits the range of permissible responses and prefigures the character of possible outcomes" (Shulman, 1986, p. 3).

Consistent with this view, he argues that traditional research is one possible—but limited—source of the knowledge base of teaching:

> The results of research on effective teaching, while valuable, are not the sole source of evidence on which to base a definition of the knowledge base of teaching. Those sources should be understood to be far richer and more extensive. Indeed, properly understood, the actual and potential sources for a knowledge base are so plentiful that our question should not be, "is there really much one needs to know in order to teach?" Rather, it should express our wonder at

how the extensive knowledge of teaching can be learned at all during the brief period allotted to teacher preparation. (Shulman,
1986, p. 7)

From this standpoint, the "wisdom of practice" represented in
efforts to design curricula, to identify fertile problems and opportunities for learning, and to ascertain the extent to which students are
developing new understandings, is a vast, untapped resource. Therefore it is essential that the knowledge base of teaching be expanded
to encompass the expertise of teachers—including teachers in elementary and secondary schools, individuals normally not considered scholars.

Building on these views, Shulman and his colleagues have developed new lines of inquiry into teaching—examining, for example, how teachers develop their subject matter knowledge—and
championed the use of new methods for doing so, such as the use of
cases. Shulman has also supported the development of the National
Board for Professional Teaching Standards, which he views as a
means of both representing a broad and rich knowledge base for
teaching and collecting some of the expertise of teachers. In more
recent work with Pat Hutchings and other colleagues in higher education, he has attempted to support the development of a scholarship of teaching as a means for faculty to articulate their knowledge
and understanding of teaching with their peers through the use of
vehicles like the course portfolio. Thus, rather than beginning with
changes in policies and the systems of rewards and incentives, Shulman advocates expanding our conception of the knowledge base of
teaching on which those policies and systems are based. In the process, instead of focusing on broadening the range of activities for
which scholars are rewarded, Shulman focuses on expanding conceptions of what kinds of people can be scholars and developing new
means to enable them to contribute to our growing knowledge base.

In sum, when used in the Boyer sense, the scholarship of teaching emphasizes the fact that teaching, like research, integration, and
application, can be a scholarly act when it is carried out thought-

fully, ethically, and effectively in ways that make the knowledge of the disciplines available to others. When used in the Shulman sense, the scholarship of teaching emphasizes that the products and activities that help to articulate, review, and exchange the expertise of teachers are as important to our knowledge and understanding of teaching as traditional modes of research and scholarship. While these views are complementary, pursuing the goals of one will not necessarily accomplish the goals of the other. Thus, even if colleges and universities around the country adopt the "Boyer model," the knowledge base of teaching will not necessarily expand. Similarly, focusing on developing new means for articulating and exchanging the knowledge of teachers at all levels might not help to validate the other important activities, such as service to the community or the ability to develop useful applications, that are also the focus of *Scholarship Reconsidered* and *Scholarship Assessed*. Furthermore, some may fear that encouraging teachers to inquire into their own practice and rewarding them for it may only reinforce the current preoccupation with research and publication, without supporting or recognizing effective teaching per se. But, whatever its roots, the scholarship of teaching can serve as a vehicle for improving the quality, effectiveness, and status of teaching—and both expanding the knowledge base and rethinking reward systems are central to this purpose.

The Scholarship of Teaching Today

In the view put forward here, questions about the form and quality of the scholarship of teaching cannot be answered a priori or in the abstract. The answers will emerge out of the efforts to articulate, examine, and share the understandings and expertise teachers need to carry out their practice. It is those efforts that will lead to the development of a new form of scholarship that expands our ideas about what kinds of products "count" and takes into consideration the demands and opportunities that arise when teachers endeavor to create, examine, and use those products.

Although the advancement of knowledge in teaching does not have to rely solely on the production of traditional investigations of teaching submitted to formal processes of peer review, every teacher and student can benefit from an educational system in which teachers critically examine and build on the work and ideas of their colleagues. This approach presumes that efforts to develop the scholarship of teaching involve a wide range of activities that can improve the quality and status of teaching on a larger scale, including:

- Producing ideas and products and prompting discussions that stimulate and inform teachers' efforts to reflect on and inquire into their own practice
- Developing methods of documentation and different kinds of products that can be used by teachers who wish to reflect on their own practice
- Establishing the language and mechanisms that can support the review and exchange of the methods and results of inquiries of all kinds
- Creating the institutional supports so that teachers can get the time and resources they need to reflect on and improve their practice
- Building public understanding that teaching is a complex endeavor in which personal reflection as well as scholarly inquiry are essential to improvements in student learning and the development of effective teachers

But from this perspective, there can be no scholarship of teaching—and no advancement of teaching—without concrete and common records of what teachers do to support student learning, and without means and mechanisms for teachers to make their teaching public and to examine and to exchange what they are learning with others.

1

INTRODUCTION

Bringing Teaching Out of the Shadows

It is a fantasy, in some respects, to imagine that many people could see the work that students and teachers do in school and college classrooms or that faculty members could freely and happily exchange and discuss their work in person, in publications, or through the Internet. These remain fantasies today for a host of reasons: insufficient time, lack of resources, and limited access to technology; stubborn bureaucracies; and school cultures that reward conformity rather than creativity. Nonetheless, we can imagine what such a public system would look like and what the implications would be for students, teachers, administrators, and parents.

Putting the "Public" Back into Public Education

In a system that makes teaching public, what happens in classrooms is no longer a mystery. Teachers work together, sharing their expertise with colleagues in their own communities and across the country, and contributing to the development of a rigorously examined and constructively debated body of knowledge. Teachers from all levels, kindergarten through the Ph.D. seminar, learn from both the commonalities and the significant differences in the work of teaching that they do. Administrators and policymakers look at samples of student work from their own campuses and others, identify promising instructional innovations, and provide support targeted to the strengths and needs they see in their students and their faculty. Parents and members of the wider public can see what their children are doing in school, and they have opportunities to develop their understanding of both how well the children are doing and *why* they are or are not doing well. By making teaching public, the emphasis can be shifted from political accountability to public responsibility. Making such a shift, however, depends on confronting both long-standing efforts to monitor teachers and their work and pervasive assumptions about the simplicity of teaching that undermine investments in the time and resources teachers need to develop and share their expertise.

Overseen and Overlooked

Although numerous initiatives over the last century have focused on making public education accessible to everyone, the ability to see what goes on in the name of public education remains limited. Ever since Americans created the one-room schoolhouse and sent their children to it, formal education has taken place behind closed doors. In the early days of public schooling in the United States, local communities could keep a close watch and a tight rein on education by hiring, monitoring, and firing the schoolmaster (Tyack, 1974). The task may have been made easier by the fact that communities were smaller and schoolmasters could be judged on the basis of their public deportment. In a sense, community members did not have to see into the classroom to feel they knew what the teacher was doing.

As communities grew and the task of compulsory education in cities and other communities became more and more complex, communities turned to principals and superintendents to oversee and manage the work of teachers, and the development and approval of textbooks for use in many schools and communities and the explosion in the use of tests and testing early in the twentieth century provided further means to control what went on in classrooms without having to go into them.

Occasionally, often-horrified critics peered into schools to "discover" what really goes on and report it to the public (see Kozol,

1967, for example), but for the most part, over the last thirty years we have relied on test score data or other secondary sources to judge the state of education and, by implication, the work and effectiveness of teachers. We have tried to refine accountability systems by specifying more carefully what should be taught and testing more vigorously. We have invented new tests, administered them to more students more often, and attached greater consequences to the results.

Even today, as educators, policymakers, and the business community continue to launch efforts to raise standards, invent better curricula, implement "research-based" practices, and improve teacher preparation and professional development, few reform efforts reach directly into the classroom to look carefully at what teachers do. This situation is as true in colleges and universities as it is in elementary and high schools. Across the country, from kindergarten classrooms to Ph.D. seminars, we rely on relatively superficial measures to determine whether or not teachers and students are doing well. If the students are engaged (or at least quiet), test scores are high, grades good, and student evaluations strong, we assume that the class is going well, the teachers are good, and learning is taking place. But if students are active and noisy, if the scores are low, grades bad, and student evaluations weak, we assume that something's wrong, the teachers are not qualified, and learning is not taking place. However, few people—inside or outside education—have a particularly well-developed sense of the many different kinds of classroom arrangements and activities that can support student learning, and few can merely observe a class, look at a syllabus, or even review a piece of student work and determine whether or not sufficient learning is taking place.

Of course, surface indicators such as grades and test scores serve a useful and necessary purpose. They allow quick, general comparisons across students and schools. At the same time, they can be misleading. In particular, they represent teaching and learning as if the playing field is level. They provide little of the contextual information that is needed to adequately interpret those results, and in the process they suggest that context does not matter. In the world of surface indicators, teaching in a well-supported school in a wealthy area is considered to be the same as teaching in a school with limited resources in an impoverished neighborhood.

Furthermore, surface indicators really only tell us what it *looks like* is going on. In many cases those surface indicators may not tell the whole story. Stories about schools where students were getting good grades and seemed to be learning—but the truth turned out to be otherwise—are well known. Zavala Elementary School in Austin Texas, for example, launched a major reform effort after the principal called parents and teachers together and showed them that even though most of the students were getting good grades, many were failing on standardized tests (Murnane & Levy, 1996; Shirley, 1997). Even studies conducted with students and graduates at Harvard and MIT have shown that some students who have performed well in classes and tests in math and science leave class unable to apply their learning in common tasks such as explaining the phases of the moon (Gardner, 1991). It is as if, when trying to figure out how well a car is running, we do not bother to look under the hood.

Why Make Teaching Public?

The invisibility of teaching and the focus on overseeing teachers' work grow out of the persistent and prevailing assumptions that teaching is a relatively simple process, one that requires little more than basic skills and can be studied largely without reference to the expertise of teachers themselves. Such views fail to take into account the extent to which high-quality teaching has to be adapted to the demands of constantly evolving curricula, changing contexts, shifting demographics, and the varying strengths and needs of students (Ball, 1996; Lampert, 2001).

It is possible to imagine teachers who feel their lesson plans and curricula are so well developed, their strategies for classroom practice so refined, and their skills in interacting with students so effective that they can carry out their work almost without thinking about it. Like chess masters who have seen all the moves and know how all the games turn out, their practice has reached such a level of mastery that they can act intuitively, recognize problems auto-matically, and make appropriate responses with ease (Berliner, 1988). However, substantial differences exist between logical, con-crete games like chess and an inherently ambiguous and unpre-dictable craft like teaching (Shulman, 1987; Lampert, 1985; Ball, 1996; McDonald, 1992). Teachers also must deal with the fact that conceptions of what and how students learn keep changing. These changes come about through the development of knowledge in the subject matter disciplines such as mathematics, English, and history; the development of new pedagogical approaches and techniques; and changes in policies, programs, and textbooks that are intended to help to guide teachers' instruction in the classroom. Correspond-ingly, over the years teachers have to make adjustments in their strategies and approaches to meet the needs and interests of chang-ing student populations. Furthermore, at any given time classroom activity and student learning are open to interpretation (Eisner, 1998). What one teacher sees in a situation or in one student may be quite different from what others see, and, accordingly, they may re-spond in very different ways. Finally, the outcomes of teaching are unclear. Even with higher standards and better tests, teachers can-not be sure exactly what students will be doing in the future or that what students do in the classroom in one day or in one year will necessarily lead them to behave appropriately or act successfully in related situations in the future.

In a way, what teachers have to do is akin to playing twenty (or thirty or forty) games of chess all at once. To complicate matters, teachers cannot see all the pieces on each of the boards, and they often have to make the same move in every game (regardless of the progress of the individual matches). And teachers always pick up the game in the middle: they have to build on the "moves" of their colleagues and then pass the game on to others. Under these cir-cumstances, mastering a finite set of moves or strategies or imple-menting a preordained script is not sufficient; teachers need to develop the ability to make professional judgments with limited information in uncertain environments. In doing so, teachers gain knowledge and understanding of the process of learning that others are unlikely to have and that are not easily captured in research or experiments that attempt to generalize across groups and settings. This expertise—grounded in specific situations and adapted to the needs of particular students and communities—needs to be articulated, examined, and shared.

Why Is Making Teaching Public So Hard?

Assumptions About the Nature and Work of Teaching

Limited time and rewards for reflecting on their practice and sharing it with others often leaves teachers with few regular opportunities to reflect on their work or share what they are doing in their own schools, much less with colleagues in other communities (Little, 1999, 1990; Lortie, 1975; Rosenholtz, 1989). As a consequence, many teachers lack the means and the support they need to adapt their practice to the changing conditions they constantly face or to consciously and purposely deepen their expertise and produce more sophisticated performances.

The lack of support for teachers' learning stands in marked contrast to the elaborate and sophisticated support systems that can help professionals in other fields to develop their ideas and share them with a wide range of audiences. Nowhere are these differences in support more evident than in comparing the treatment of artists and scholars with the treatment of teachers. "Uninterrupted time to work, good working conditions, and a supportive community"—that is the promise of many institutions dedicated to advancing the work of scholars and artists. In institutions for advanced study, scholars and artists learn when they work alone and without interruption, with little or no guidance from others, in a beautiful environment and a relaxed social setting; but teachers usually learn in intense courses, seminars, and workshops, in close collaboration with peers, and under the supervision of someone else (Hatch, 1998).

These drastically different approaches to the support of scholars, artists, and teachers are rooted in strikingly different perceptions of the outcomes and nature of the work that teachers and artists and scholars do and in substantial differences in the conditions and contexts in which their work is carried out. Both these differences in perceptions and contexts help to explain why there has been so little support to help make teaching public.

Advancing the Field Versus Developing Personal Skills

Advanced study programs for artists and scholars reflect the basic premise that the *work* of artists and scholars has a life beyond the individual that will make a difference in their fields and disciplines. In contrast, programs for teachers are based on the premise that the *individual* will make a difference in the lives of others. Thus many programs for artists and scholars assume that those who have been selected have the skills, expertise, and potential to make those contributions. And if those individuals need anything to advance the field (aside from time to do their own work), these programs suggest that what they need primarily is supportive and stimulating interaction with peers with whom they might not ordinarily come into contact. Consistent with these beliefs, it would be presumptuous for directors or staff to assume that they knew what the participants needed to make their breakthroughs and that programming particular activities would be counterproductive. However, programs for teachers make the assumption that, no matter how skilled and accomplished the participants are, they could be more effective if they could learn the latest ideas, techniques, or strategies developed by other experts. As a result, it makes sense to engage them explicitly in activities in which they can learn with and from others.

Doing Creative Work Versus Learning to Improve

Hand in hand with such different premises are basic differences in the way the work that artists and scholars do and the work that teachers do is perceived. "Real work" for scholars and artists includes the examination, development, and refinement of the ideas and products that reflect their art and scholarship. Although many of these individuals may also teach, teaching is usually part of the daily burden of activities from which they are relieved. In contrast, many people view the "real work" of teachers as taking place solely in the classroom in interactions with students. Work that takes place outside the classroom—whether for planning, professional development, or building relationships with colleagues and parents—is often seen as secondary (if it is considered to be work at all).

As a consequence of these different perceptions, when scholars and artists go to centers for advanced study, they are perceived as going to do their real work and getting away from the distractions and other burdens that can interfere with it; but when teachers take time out from their own classrooms, they often have to face the perception that they are getting a break from their work and from their primary responsibilities.

Working in a Public, Historical Context Versus Working in Isolated Places

The differences in advanced study programs also grow from the different conditions in which the work of artists and scholars and that of teachers is carried out. For example, although it is not always easy for young and unknown artists and scholars to get their works displayed, produced, or published, it is expected that they will do so. In areas such as the visual arts, music, and drama, professionals have the means to make their work and ideas public in galleries, museums, theaters, journals, and books. Scholars can choose from a wide array of informal lunches, job talks, meetings, presentations, conference proceedings, and publication opportunities to share their latest research with their peers. Publishing industries and institutions exist that can make their work public.

Furthermore, the fact that artists and scholars produce works that can last over time and that can be read and viewed by wide audiences creates a history to which the participants in centers for artists and scholars can contribute. Even something as simple as the fact that the previous residents have left their signatures on the walls of their studios at an artists' retreat like Yaddo in Saratoga Springs, New York, can have a profound effect in this context. As the public affairs coordinator from Yaddo once explained to me, "I showed [a writer] into her studio and a couple of days later she said that she remembers very clearly the moment in her life when she decided she was going to be a writer, and it was after she'd just completed a book by James Baldwin. And she's sitting there working on her novel in the studio and she looks up and sees James Baldwin's name signed on the pine board on the wall." Because many of the most recognized and accomplished scholars and artists have been to centers like these, to be a resident is, in some ways, to join with them. In such settings, James Baldwin becomes a colleague and not just an inspiration.

Given these conditions, programs for artists and scholars assume that they must give artists the time and place to do the *real* work—doing research and creating art—that they have the capacity to do but may not be able to do because of the normal constraints of their daily lives. Correspondingly, programs for scholars and artists generally make little effort to find out how the participants' work is going while they are in residence. At most, program staff may ask participants to report on what they have done during their residencies, or they may keep track of the products produced by participants; rarely are the programs themselves asked or expected to produce results that demonstrate the value of their efforts.

Instead, program staff assume that if they provide the time and place, then the results will come. Books will be published, articles will be read, artwork will be displayed, and plays and music will be performed. It's assumed that simply by placing artists and scholars in proximity to one another they can become part of a larger community; they can make connections to existing networks and gain access to the publishers, editors, producers, and funders they might need for support. Simply by being in the same surroundings as James Baldwin, Aaron Copland, and Albert Einstein, they can become a part of the history—and the future—of their professions.

Immediate Impact Versus Long-Term Development

The conditions for teachers are far different. In programs for teachers, the focus is on the here and now, and they are expected to develop skills that will have immediate benefits for their students. As a consequence, teachers face almost constant assessments of their own work or that of their students, and programs for teachers are often asked to pursue formal evaluations and produce quantitative results that show what the participants have learned and demonstrate the "added value" of the programs immediately after teachers have participated.

Furthermore, there are few expectations that teachers will produce work that will be shared beyond their classes and schools, and, in comparison with artists and scholars, relatively few means exist for teachers to publish their work and share it widely. The industries and institutions of education are designed to provide teachers with materials and information and to test them on what they do with it, not to help them share their own work with a wider audience. Some teachers can and do write articles and books, and there are some journals and book series dedicated specifically to publishing the work of teachers, but for the most part these opportunities remain few and far between, and for most people these activities are generally secondary to their real work—teaching.

Instead, what is shared widely is the work *on teaching*—produced to a large extent by researchers and others—rather then the work *by teachers*. It is as if, in the art world, there were a vast network to support the development and dissemination of the work of the philosophers, reviewers, and critics, but few ways for painters, writers, sculptors, and musicians to get out of their studios and share the products of their work with their peers or a wider audience.

Due to the absence of an infrastructure analogous to the one that supports the development, dissemination, and preservation of the work of artists and scholars, it is as if teaching has no history. Although artists and scholars, and even the public at large, know the names of many of the most accomplished members of art and academia, even teachers are more likely to know the names of famous researchers than they are to know the names of effective teachers. Artists and scholars can trace their work back to the influences of people they never met or knew, but many teachers are rooted in the present. Their horizons are largely restricted to the teachers they have had in their own experiences and to the peers that they meet in their own schools and communities.

Bringing Teaching Out of the Shadows

Despite the different assumptions that underlie the treatment of teachers and the treatment of artists, scholars, and other professionals and the corresponding challenges for making teaching public, well-established efforts to support teacher inquiry and research among K–12 educators and more recent initiatives to enable higher education faculty to document and examine their classroom practice reflect an entirely different set of beliefs (see, for example, Cochran-Smith & Lytle, 1993; Freedman, 1999; Stenhouse, 1983, 1988; Hollingsworth & Sockett, 1994). Building on Dewey's (1904) view that learning to teach is inseparable from learning to inquire, these efforts approach teaching as a complex intellectual endeavor that demands disciplinary expertise, a deep understanding of students, and sophisticated pedagogical skills. Furthermore, these efforts reflect the belief that the skills of the teacher are not innate capacities, but abilities that need to be developed over time, in collaboration with others. In this view, teachers are gaining new insights and ideas and learning all the time, advancing not only their own work but also the work of their colleagues and their disciplines (Hatch, 2005).

These continuing efforts, along with renewed interest in education and recent developments in schools and college campuses across the country, provide glimmers of hope that the time may be right for change:

- Although many teachers continue to teach behind closed doors, on some schools and on college campuses they now meet regularly to share and discuss student work, write cases about their experiences, visit one another's classrooms, and post assignments and course materials on websites.

- Whereas professional development for K–12 teachers once consisted largely of brief "in service" workshops, and most professors had no preparation or professional development for teaching at all, faculty in both K–12 and higher education now have some opportunities to participate in discussion groups, teaching circles, video clubs, and "lesson studies" that enable them to learn from and build upon one another's work.

- Whereas the quality of teaching was once assessed by simple checklists and student evaluations—or ignored entirely— some teachers and higher education faculty now create their own portfolios, participate in peer review projects, and develop the skills to document their practice, reflect upon it, and improve it.

- Advances in technology and the reality that more and more of the materials and interactions of teaching and learning can be made available through the Internet are also contributing to an unprecedented opportunity to develop more sophisticated ways to collect, examine, and share the work of teaching and learning.

These developments reflect, as well, the growth of a number of institutions and organizations—including school reform networks, district-based professional development centers, campus-based centers for teaching and learning, and virtual networks—that are beginning to establish some of the incentives, infrastructure, and support that teachers need to make their work public.

The success of these endeavors rests on addressing the basic assumptions that lead society to treat teachers so differently from the way in which artists, scholars, and other professionals are treated. In particular, we must come to terms with history. A history of teaching should reflect in a central way the breakthroughs, debates, and advances of many different teachers. To make history, teachers have to have the kinds of institutional supports and networks that preserve ideas and advances in other fields. That means that simply giving teachers more time and space for reflecting on and articulating their expertise is not sufficient; we have to build an infrastructure for the scholarship of teaching by developing new means for representation and publication and by establishing forums for the discussion and exchange of teaching to which many teachers and the wider public can have access. We can begin to build that infrastructure by looking carefully at what it takes for teachers to make their teaching public and at how and what they learn when they do.

Questions for Consideration

What assumptions do people make about teaching?

How hard is it to learn to teach? Is it a "natural" process" or one requiring teachers to develop specialized skills and knowledge?

How does the work of teachers compare to the work of other professionals? To the work of scholars and artists?

What will it take to make teaching public?

2

IN THE CLASSROOM

Challenges and Opportunities
for Learning from Teaching

Educators often blame structural problems—such as lack of time and rewards—for preventing K–12 teachers from reflecting on their work. But when it comes to the scholarship of teaching and other efforts to make teaching public, the problems go even deeper. Scholarship and the advancement of knowledge in most disciplines depend on the freedom to think, to inquire, and to express one's unique views and perspective. Yet teachers are constrained by a variety of conceptual, methodological, and contextual problems that limit not only *when* they can document, examine, and discuss their own work and the work of their colleagues, but also *how* they can think about it. First, the practical demands and personal investments of classroom practice make it extremely difficult for teachers to develop and maintain the kind of neutrality and distance associated with some forms of scholarship. Second, many K–12 teachers cannot take advantage of the vast infrastructure that supports the development and the informal and formal exchange of scholarship—including means of sharing methods; acquiring relevant skills; and publishing, presenting, and critiquing results—that is available to those who work in higher education. Third, the context and cultures of teaching provide neither the stability nor the collegial relationships needed to make the interpretation of classroom practice a regular source for the advancement of knowledge and new ideas.

The experiences of three teachers who participated in the first cohort of the CASTL program for elementary and secondary teachers—Marlene Carter, Stan Hitomi, and Mary Hurley—

illuminate key aspects of these conceptual, methodological, and contextual problems. Their cases are particularly instructive because they demonstrate the depth and complexity of the problems that even teachers skilled in both teaching and inquiry have to face. All have been involved in a variety of documentation efforts and have received some support and rewards for their efforts. Yet even these teachers have had to deal with numerous constraints on their opportunities to develop their work in ways that will enable others to build upon it.

Carter, a high school English teacher who teaches Advanced Placement (AP) courses at a magnet high school in inner-city Los Angeles, sought to understand why many of her African-American male students do not do as well as either she believes they can or they believe they can (Carter, 2005). Her efforts as a Carnegie scholar show how difficult it can be to conceive of a straightforward, systematic study when the demands of teaching and the needs of her students are always shifting, and when her own goals and actions are parts of the subject in question.

At the time of Hitomi's participation in CASTL, he taught science classes and served as a technology coordinator in a suburban high school in California's San Francisco Bay Area. His study examined how students can use a technique called *concept-mapping* to help them develop a robust understanding of key scientific ideas. His work highlights the ongoing struggle to find or develop inquiry methods that are both appropriate to the classroom context and considered legitimate for research outside that context.

In 1997–1999, Hurley was a kindergarten and first grade teacher at a magnet school in Oakland, California. Hurley sought to document her efforts to revise and improve just one daily activity in her own classroom—"author's chair"—asking, "What does it take to make this one, brief [15-minute] activity a successful and engaging learning experience for students?" In the process, Hurley's experience demonstrates how the conventions and cultures of teaching—even for teachers and schools committed to inquiry and reform—can make it almost impossible to maintain a focus on a research project and to carry out that project in between classes, around reform ef-forts, and in the midst of the normal demands of life.

Despite these problems, the experiences of these three teachers also provide demonstration cases that teachers can meet these chal-lenges and produce public inquiries. The results of their investiga-tions were produced in formats ranging from traditional articles to websites and videos, and their experiences point the way for us to consider the kinds of support and the kinds of changes in K–12 schools in particular that could encourage teachers to make their work public and contribute to the advancement of the profession as a whole.

Dealing with the Complexities of Teaching

"I have a problem," Carter announces to a small group of col-leagues. Over the past year and half Carter has been meeting with this group periodically to discuss her study of the underachievement of African-American male students in her AP English class. "Al-though the boys in the class in the last several years really didn't seem to be doing as well as they could," she continues, "this year, both the boys and the girls are really doing well."

Most teachers would love to have Carter's "problem." But al-though the improvement in the students' performance this year is exactly what a teacher like Carter would like to see, from her per-spective as a researcher the improvement means that the basic na-ture of her study has to change. In the previous year, she examined the factors in the students' lives that might contribute to their un-derachievement, and this year she was planning to document how her teaching practices might help them improve their performance. However, since the young men began the year performing at a much higher level than their peers in the past, she immediately had to devise a new plan for her research to take into account this happy, but unanticipated, turn of events.

Of course, all researchers are presented with such "problems" and opportunities. And Carter can make adjustments. She can shift

her focus so that, instead of documenting how her teaching practices might help these students, she can look at the factors that may
have helped these students in previous years. But she has to make
these adjustments at the same time that she refines her curriculum
so that it meets the needs of this year's group of students and at the
same time so that she deals with all the usual requirements of teaching. And, appropriately, her teaching demands her primary attention. She can make decisions about what questions to examine and
how and when to study them only in the context of what is likely
to be best for her students and her classroom right now. As Stan
Hitomi puts it, her research is like a trailer that is hitched onto the
back of her classroom practice: it can only go where her teaching
can take it.

Although teachers can provide a perspective on their teaching
and their students' learning that traditional researchers often cannot, the fact that the demands of teaching must take precedence
over the demands of research makes it particularly difficult for teachers to maintain a focus on a particular issue or question. For teachers,
the object of study is like a moving target that refuses to stay still
long enough to get a careful look: the more carefully teachers look
at their practice, the more they see things to fix, and as teachers
they are responsible for responding to what they see and making the
necessary changes.

Furthermore, teachers necessarily have to take into account
everything that happens in the classroom (and often outside of it as
well). In a sense, which aspect of their practice is most successful or
effective is much less important than the fact that the sum total of
their efforts leads to positive outcomes. Yet many kinds of conventional scholarship demand that researchers isolate and break down
variables; understanding *how* the process works contributes to the
advancement of knowledge and therefore has to take precedence
over whether or not positive outcomes are achieved. As a result, it
is not surprising that teachers like Carter are reluctant to focus their
inquiries on a small set of variables. She knows that numerous factors may contribute to the performance of the young men in her

class—including previous classroom experiences, family support, and participation in sports and extracurricular activities—and she has to be prepared to take all of these into account in order to teach her students well.

Similarly, although conventional research demands a kind of neutrality or distance from the object of study, teachers cannot escape from the fact that when they pursue questions in their own classroom, in some ways their own actions, beliefs, and passions are in question as well. For Carter, this means that even as she explores the positive and negative impact of factors such as participation in sports and student motivation on their performance, she also has to ask what contribution she might be making to the problem. Might there be another approach, or perhaps another person, who could be more effective with these students? Entertaining such doubts may be especially difficult when teachers need to rely on faith and confidence to sustain themselves through both the disappointments and the achievements that are experienced with any group of students.

In part, the CASTL scholars deal with these challenges by accepting them. These tensions between the passions and complexities of teaching and the demands of conventional research are givens. But the teachers also address these problems by making the evolution of practice a key focus for study rather than a variable that has to be controlled. Carter's study does not simply focus on whether or not a particular technique or approach might work more effectively with her male students; her study chronicles her investigation into students' backgrounds, her growing understanding of the phenomenon, and both the successes and the failures of her efforts to respond in the classroom to what she's learning.

For those who inquire into their own teaching, responding to these challenges also means building on the passions in their practice. By choosing questions that are deeply meaningful to them but that also have the potential to be of interest to a wide audience, these teachers can sustain the interest and energy they need to remain committed to and focused on their investigations at the same time that they remain committed to their students. Thus, for Carter, studying the underachievement of African-American males in her class is not just a pedagogical concern: as an African-American woman and the mother of two young boys, she is concerned about the implications for her as a parent and as a member of the larger African-American and educational communities. As she put it in a description of how she came to focus her work on the issue of underachievement:

> I turned this issue over in my mind and talked about it with two close friends of mine. Both are mothers of African-American sons and both are teachers. We discussed the research we had read on how school systems do not meet the needs of African-American males. We also shared stories of how most teachers seemed to mis-understand our sons, how disappointed we are in the system, and how we would like to see the system change. As we talked, I felt that I had to be part of that change. Since young men were not succeed-ing in my class, I needed to make some changes in my curriculum, strategies, and attitudes in order to be a more effective teacher. In addition, I knew that I was not the only one who had to do some changing. I wondered how I could help my students (and my own son) take more of an interest in their academic education and have a more positive attitude toward learning.

For Carter, developing an understanding of the problem that goes far beyond her classroom and her teaching helps to sustain her even if it leads her to doubt some aspects of what she does.

Finding Space and Support for Examining Teaching

Hitomi projects an image from his computer onto the wall of a small seminar room. Four colleagues, seated around the table, ex-amine the illumination of one student's efforts to use a concept map to explain how viruses spread. Hitomi talks quickly and with some concern. Throughout his efforts to document how technology can assist students—particularly students labeled as having special learning needs—in developing these maps, he has been worried about the most appropriate methods to use:

> This [work] is such an out-of-the-box thing for me that, from day to day—unless I'm sitting really quietly for two or three hours—I'm terribly confused. For example, my case study is one or two individuals. But could the whole class be a case study? Or could a whole school be a case study? And the answer comes back "yes." And then, you have to go back and think it through, because you've said that and know it's true, but now you have to look at how it could be a case study, you know what I mean?

As a scientist, Hitomi knows well the process and methods of scientific research. This background is crucial to his effectiveness as a teacher of biology and chemistry, but it also contributes to his struggles to come to grips with an appropriate set of methods for inquiring into his own practice. Hitomi knows the dangers of generalizing from the results of case studies. He also knows that his fellow science teachers and many of the colleagues he works with at Lawrence Livermore Labs are likely to view his work through the lens of the traditional experimental sciences. But that process—one defined by hypothesis testing, sampling, and experimental control—does not suit the kinds of questions he wants to pursue with his own class. For one thing, how can he relegate some students to a "control" group that cannot use the concept-mapping technique or related computer software if he truly believes, as his previous experience suggests, that it is a better way to teach?

For Hitomi, departing from the tried-and-true experimental methods requires him to make a kind of psychological break from the mind-set he shares with colleagues and friends. But even teachers without a background in the "hard" sciences are aware of standards for quality scientific research and must grapple with fears that their own work will be dismissed if they do not use rigorous scientific methods. In fact, particularly in the early stages of their inquiries, teachers like Hitomi and Carter may take a narrow view of what counts as science and scholarship. They seem to feel compelled to develop a testable hypothesis, to figure out ways to compare groups, to produce replicable outcomes, and to measure them systematically.

Many scholars have to deal with this "experimental bias," but the complex and personal nature of teaching may make it particularly difficult for teachers both to use such methods and to feel comfortable if they do not. In one discussion with her colleagues from the CASTL program, for example, Carter apologized profusely that she had not collected data from her students in a "systematic" manner. Indeed, Carter had not established a regular schedule for interviewing her male students or for recording her own reflections, but she had investigated numerous potential sources of underachievement by looking into students' family situations, previous test scores, and participation in sports. As a result, she was able to make a powerful argument that many of the conventional assumptions about why African-American male students might be underachieving did not apply to her students. Even without collecting data directly from her students "systematically," she was able to present her conclusions in a way that provoked and challenged her colleagues and others to whom she had presented her findings.

Although Hitomi and Carter continue to worry about the systematicity and rigor of their work, they and their colleagues have begun to overcome their concerns about experimental research by recognizing that there are legitimate scholarly methods better suited to research in their classrooms. A key advance for Hitomi came when he recognized that the observational research he learned about as an undergraduate in his natural science classes might serve as a better analogue for his investigations of his teaching. This recognition came as a kind of epiphany while he was studiously making notes about the class he was teaching in preparation for a pilot experiment on concept-mapping. As he explained it in an interview, "Typically in a field journal, you write down some observations and you make some interpretations of what you see and things like that, but you're not really allowed to go crazy, you know. And, suddenly, I thought, wow, what if I tried *this*?"

At another time, Hitomi noted that many natural historians keep journals with two sections: one for lots of observations without a focus and another reserved for those times when the researcher sees something in particular—a discrepant event or something that reinforces a pattern. He realized, as he put it, "This is what I should be doing in my classroom." By establishing these links between his methods of inquiry and the accepted methods of another scientific discipline, Hitomi gave himself permission to depart from traditional experimental methods. Although it was largely a mental leap to see his inquiries in terms of the natural sciences, it gave his efforts a legitimacy and rigor that he believed they had previously lacked.

Despite giving himself permission to consider a wider range of methods, however, Hitomi is still faced with the task of choosing among them. Unfortunately, however, his training as an experimental scientist has not prepared him to do case studies or to use other qualitative methods that might be more suitable for documenting his own practice. Teachers like Carter, whose work and experience are largely in the humanities, may feel even less prepared to carry out investigations into their practice; and even those faculty members who are familiar with some research methods may have had little experience in dealing with many other critical aspects of scholarship and research, like working with human subjects, obtaining informed consent, or finding outlets for publication.

These problems may be particularly pronounced for K–12 teachers who examine their own teaching. Although many faculty in higher education may not have a background in quantitative or qualitative research, they are well aware of the processes and procedures of scholarship both within their own disciplines and in academia in general. In a sense, faculty in higher education who examine their own teaching can try to take advantage of a vast infrastructure that supports the development, pursuit, and publication of research and scholarship in numerous other disciplines. That support may include opportunities for funding; informal and formal opportunities to discuss the methods, progress, and results of inquiries; and access to information about how to shape products for publication and where to publish them. Faculty in higher education who want to pursue the scholarship of teaching have to figure out how to take advantage of this infrastructure to deal with a different kind of inquiry, but most K–12 faculty have little or no connection to the infrastructure of scholarly production and presentation in the first place. Even teachers like Carter, who helps to lead the Los Angeles chapter of the National Writing Project and has access to much more support than many other teachers, have relatively few opportunities to talk to their colleagues about which methods to use, where to find relevant literature, or even where to publish outside of their own networks.

Naturally, a lack of information and support for selecting methods and for preparing materials for presentation and publication exacerbates any concerns teachers have about whether or not their work is likely to be effective and legitimate. Any interest that teachers have in going public can compound these concerns. For Hitomi, as for the rest of the CASTL scholars, the specter of going public is double layered: they are making public the process and products of their inquiry and they are making public the process and outcomes of their teaching. Thus, while most teachers are evaluated simply by the outcomes of their students, those who make their teaching— and their inquiries into it—public may open themselves to critiques of many other aspects of their work, including their choices of methods of investigation, the reliability and validity of their findings, the pedagogical decisions they make about which skills and ideas to emphasize, and the personal efforts they make to respond to their students. For example, the videotapes Hitomi makes in the process of developing case studies of several students' work on concept-mapping reveal how Hitomi interacts with those students amid the noise and excitement of classroom activity. Even though Hitomi can control which videotapes to show, he cannot be sure who will see those tapes or how they will respond. As a result, knowing that they are making the inquiries and practice public may increase the natural concerns and apprehensions that teachers have about whether they are "doing the right thing" to meet the needs of their own students and to satisfy the demands of a wider audience.

Dwelling on a lack of infrastructure for research and the pressures of going public can make the challenges of inquiring into teaching seem insurmountable. But the reality is that teachers can find and create support for their work, and, like others who are often in the public eye, they can become somewhat accustomed to the pressures. Hitomi deals with these problems head on. In fact, he has begun to build the infrastructure that he and his colleagues need to support research. At his high school, he is part of a team of teachers who are launching an academy or "school within a school" in which the entire focus is on research. Although the primary goal is to create a setting in which students regularly engage in meaningful research projects as a means of developing key skills and understandings, the academy is designed to recognize the importance of teachers engaging in their own research projects. Thus the members of the academy are striving to create time when teachers can meet together to discuss their research and to find forums in which they can present it to their students or other members of the school community. In the process, they are creating opportunities (as well as need) for discussions of appropriate methods, ethical issues such as informed consent, and the intellectual property rights of the members of the academy (including the students) in the products of their research—issues that, for many higher education faculty, are already addressed by both their institutions and scholarly societies.

Although Carter, like many teachers, has few incentives or rewards within the traditional school or district structure for examining her own teaching, the meetings and conferences of the National Writing Project provide her with natural opportunities to present what she's learning. With such opportunities come needs to write proposals, meet deadlines, and prepare summaries of work. And these demands, in turn, help to provide structure and incentives for carrying out her inquiry. Of course, for scholars in higher education, presenting their work is a normal activity, but it is out of the ordinary for many K–12 teachers. In response, Hitomi and Hurley have helped to manufacture these opportunities for themselves and their colleagues. In their role as advisors to the Center for Teaching and

Learning (an organization dedicated to communicating the needs and views of California teachers to policymakers), for example, they are helping to make the presentation and discussion of teachers' examinations of their own practice a regular part of their meetings.

Navigating the Contexts and Cultures of Teaching

Entries from Hurley's journal, stories handwritten by her K–1 students, and tapes of students' presentations to their peers are scattered across the table. Hurley has just described to a small group of CASTL scholars her efforts to document the revisions she has made to improve students' experiences and work in "author's chair." In author's chair, one or two students in her Oakland K–1 classroom read stories they have written and receive feedback from their classmates. Her examination demonstrates the ups and downs she and the students endured as she attempted to develop and refine classroom routines for writing drafts, making presentations, and giving feedback. The discussion also reveals her efforts to shape the activity both to meet the needs of students like Edie, who can barely sit still, and to challenge students like Ernesto, who are already reading and relating sophisticated stories to their peers. Her documentation efforts also provide her colleagues with a glimpse into the way that, over the course of the year, she involves her students in discussions of the activity and takes their comments into account so that they grow more and more engaged in writing and more and more committed to writing well.

After a moment, Hurley reaches into the bag that sits next to her on the floor. With both hands, she pulls out a large book the size and shape of a complete and unabridged encyclopedia. She drops it onto the table. It lands with a loud thud, displacing a few stray pieces of paper in the process. "This," she says, "is the reading curriculum that I'm supposed to implement for ninety minutes every day next year." She pauses again, then adds, "I'll have an afternoon of training in September, two days before the start of school."

To the colleagues sitting around the table, this curriculum seems to have been dropped, out of the blue, into Hurley's classroom and onto her inquiry. For Hurley, however, it is just par for the course. In fact, the curriculum is a relatively good one, and she is not entirely opposed to using it. It is just another example of the many demands and issues to which she and teachers like her have to respond. In fact, every year Hurley has to deal with predictable demands like the district's regular request to implement an entirely new curriculum in at least one subject area; she also has to deal with unpredictable events like the fact that her school has a new principal; and she must respond to the fact that she has an unusually large number of kindergarten students with significant emotional and behavioral problems. These demands of her classroom and school context eat away at any time and attention that Hurley had hoped to dedicate to her inquiry into author's chair during her first semester of work. Rather than trying to avoid or reduce these contextual problems, she and her CASTL colleagues have to expect that they will have to conduct their inquiries in the midst of school and classroom life that is often out of their control.

For Hurley, the larger problem is to find a place and a group of colleagues in which she can talk about the kinds of pedagogical and methodological issues that her study raises. Even with more time or less interference, the culture of teaching and unspoken norms about what teachers should and should not do or say make it difficult to have the kinds of conversations that Hurley, Hitomi, and Carter might enjoy. While many teachers may be concerned about feelings of isolation from other teachers, those that seek to break out of that isolation and to discuss their teaching more publicly may also have concerns about how they will be perceived by their colleagues. As Hurley explains, her efforts to talk about her CASTL study can be viewed by others as a sign that she thinks that her practice and her classroom are more important or more effective than theirs:

> You don't want to toot your own horn, because you're trying to build
> a team and because you want everybody on board. You're not going

to pull yourself out and say, "Oh, by the way, I'm doing this really neat stuff that you're not." Or, "Carnegie has sprinkled their little dust on me, my cycle of inquiry is better than your cycle of inquiry." I mean, you don't say it nor do you think it, but by saying, "Well, my work is being shared outside our circle of the school and other people are interested and care about it," there's an implied "it's better than work that's being shared internally at the school." And so you don't bring it to the table.

In terms of their relationships with principals and administrators, in a sense those who seek to examine their teaching and make it public are "damned if they do and damned if they don't." If their work seems likely to bring prestige and positive recognition to the school, administrators may well support and publicly acknowledge it; naturally, such support may exacerbate perceptions among peers that the teacher is "showing off," and it may contribute to open discussion and critique. If the work seems likely to highlight problems in the school or difficult aspects of teaching, administrators may not want to draw attention to the work or support its discussion.

Ironically, Hurley finds it difficult to talk about her CASTL study even though her own school has made enormous strides in creating an environment in which teachers can question and inquire into their classroom practices and their effectiveness as a community of educators. In fact, Hurley and her school colleagues have used a portion of a large school improvement grant to give themselves time to sit down together each week for one hundred minutes to become a community of teachers and learners. Initially, Hurley saw this new community as ideal for supporting her own research: a group of like-minded colleagues, concerned about the welfare of students and the improvement of their practice, creating a safe place to risk exploring what was going *wrong* as well as what was going *right* in her classroom. But even in this context, Hurley has found relatively few opportunities to talk specifically about the goals and methods of her own inquiry. As Hurley explained, at her school they not only have to work against the private and isolating culture of teaching in general, but they also have to find some common ground for their conversations:

"Last year, I thought it was just the lousy culture of teaching [that made it hard to talk about this work]. It's not. I think it's because many of us really do want to forge a team at school. I mean, everybody who's still in the classroom really wants to be connected to their school community, and you choose what's going to connect you and what's going to disconnect you."

In order to create that connection or common ground, Hurley and her colleagues have chosen to focus their efforts on a schoolwide inquiry into how they can produce higher learning outcomes for all their students. As a result, Hurley's inquiry, which does not directly address these questions, does not fit that easily into the common ground they have established for their joint inquiry, and it has not found a natural place in their discussions.

Conclusion

The experiences of teachers like Carter, Hitomi, and Hurley in documenting the complexities of their practice illustrate both the challenges of and the possibilities for inquiring into teaching and sharing those results with others. Even though their inquiries may distinguish them from many of their colleagues, these teachers are finding ways to meet with colleagues, share their inquiries, and stretch their thinking about their practice. Hurley's work may not fit neatly into the discussions being carried on at her school, but she still finds time to talk about her CASTL study outside of regular school activities, often with teachers involved in inquiry projects in other schools. She also takes a more active role in sharing her work within the Coalition of Essential Schools, a school reform network in which her school takes part. Among these groups and with her CASTL colleagues, numerous subjects or issues are under discussion, and, in a sense, they have found common ground in the issues of inquiry and scholarship themselves.

As Hurley suggests, she has found people within these groups who care that she is pursuing scholarly activity, regardless of whether or not they are especially knowledgeable about or interested in the particular subjects of her work. She says,

"Caring [is not the same as interest]. Caring means that people want me to learn, people want to see me grow as a person and not get discouraged and not lose hope. . . . Interest just doesn't hold it for sustained work. For looking at it and saying, "I've got fifteen tapes, I've got to choose five to transcribe, and I can't decide and I'm way behind and I'm stuck.""

This kind of shared concern for the welfare of the teacher and belief in the value of their activity may be particularly important for those who seek to make their practice public. After all, they are under no obligation to inquire into their practice. They do not need to raise questions about their own effectiveness, and they do not have to subject the process as well as the outcomes of their work to public scrutiny. But they are willing to take that risk. As they come to know each other and their work, and as they take their teaching public, teachers like Hurley, Carter, and Hitomi are beginning to recognize that they are not alone. This sense of shared commitment may provide some of the support they need to build—or imagine— the cultures and communities that will ultimately sustain the work.

Questions for Consideration

What factors constrain teachers' learning?

How can teachers reconcile the different priorities of research and teaching?

Where can teachers find support for efforts to make their teaching public?

3

BEYOND THE CLASSROOM

How One Teacher's Inquiry
Can Influence Her Peers

When Sarah Capitelli, a member of the second cohort of CASTL scholars, graduated from her teacher education program in the spring of 1998, she felt prepared. As she put it: "I entered the profession with what I assumed was a collection of tools ready to take on a public school classroom. I had a strong theoretical foundation that was grounded in constructivist learning theory. I had some experience working with second language learners and many hours of reflection and debriefing on this experience. I felt prepared and confident with issues of classroom management and discipline."

Despite these initial perceptions, as soon as she took over her own first-second grade classroom at Manzanita, a bilingual elementary school in the San Francisco Bay Area, Capitelli's feelings about her preparation changed dramatically. "My preparation and the tools that I brought with me to my first years of teaching made little to no sense in the context in which I put myself," she wrote in a reflection during her third year of teaching. In an interview, she was even more forthright: "Nothing," she reported. "I came with absolutely nothing."

Over the next four years, Capitelli tried to get a better understanding of her frustrations. She participated in a variety of activities in which she documented her teaching, and she experimented with a variety of different classroom strategies to improve her instruction. Gradually, her concerns shifted from a focus on her own lack of skills to questions about her own perceptions of the students' use of language and the effectiveness of an "English-only" rule that the school had established for English Language Development (ELD) hour and the school's policy requiring differentiated ELD instruction for students with different levels of proficiency in English. As a result of these developments in her thinking, Capitelli began to imagine and hypothesize how she might be able to improve her practice as well as ELD instruction throughout the school.

Capitelli's experiences examining her teaching during the ELD hour illustrate what teachers often have to learn on the job, how they learn, and the roles that informal inquiries as well as more formal research and scholarship can play in the process. In particular, her experiences highlight how teachers recognize and develop new ideas and strategies in their classroom practice, how they encode and remember those ideas and strategies, and how they and their colleagues apply those ideas and strategies in new situations.

Background

After beginning her career teaching English at a school in Venezuela, Capitelli gained her certification as an elementary bilingual teacher at a small, highly regarded teacher education program in the Bay Area. (In addition to its reputation for producing well-prepared graduates, the program is also known for its emphases on support for teacher inquiry and on social justice.) After she graduated, she was hired as a first-second grade teacher in the bilingual program at Manzanita Elementary School, the same school where she served as a student teacher.

Manzanita has a student population of primarily Latino (79 percent) English Language learners (80 percent), with a small number of African-American students (12 percent) and Asian students (5 percent). As part of the bilingual program, Capitelli was responsible for teaching one hour of ELD four afternoons a week. The ELD hour was the one hour each day in which instruction was expected to be entirely in English. In that hour, Capitelli was assigned to work with the least proficient English speakers in all the first-second grade classes.[1]

Despite the general lack of support for teachers like her to inquire into their teaching, Capitelli—like Carter, Hitomi, and Hurley, her predecessors in the CASTL program—found a variety of venues both inside and outside Manzanita in which she could document her teaching, solicit the advice and feedback of her peers, and, ultimately, make public her scholarship and her developing insights about English instruction in her classroom. In particular, she benefited from the fact that Manzanita had been involved in a number of reform efforts over the previous ten years, including the development of school-wide inquiry projects as a form of professional development. As part of her involvement in those inquiry projects, Capitelli contributed to a multiyear effort to examine the process and outcomes of their English instruction. Through connections she developed in her teacher preparation program, she also joined in quarterly meetings of a regional teacher inquiry network in which she produced narratives about her practice and shared her concerns with other teachers. In the middle of her third year, she joined CASTL. As part of that program, she spent nine days during the summer in which she worked on her own to review report cards and student work she had brought with her, talked about her ELD class with other CASTL scholars, and articulated and presented what she was learning in informal groups and in brief written reports on her project.

From Hunches to Hypotheses

Learning to Improve Practice

Learning refers to the process of acquiring new information, knowledge, skills, or behaviors that leads to changes in the state, skills, or activities of an individual, group, or organization. In this view, fleeting recognition or momentary accomplishments do not constitute learning. Learning is demonstrated when new knowledge, skills, or behaviors are developed and used with some consistency. Capitelli's learning is reflected in two significant shifts in her approach to teaching in ELD hour—from instruction solely in English to instruction in English and Spanish and from instruction that focuses on the students who are "least proficient" in English to instruction with a mixed-ability group—that resulted from a series of inquires into her classroom practice over her first four years of full-time teaching (see Table 3.1).

Years One and Two (1998-2000)

English Only

During her first two years as a full-time teacher at Manzanita, Capitelli holds fast to a school-wide expectation that all instruction during ELD hour will take place in English. In the process, she focuses on trying to get her students to speak in English and becomes more and more frustrated with her inability to do so. As she writes in a narrative she produces as part of her participation in a local teacher inquiry group:

Table 3.1. Timeline of Capitelli's Work at Manzanita.

1997–1998	Student teacher in bilingual program at Manzanita (but does not work in tracked ELD program).
1998–2000	First- and second-year teacher, bilingual program, ELD instructor (one hour, four afternoons, in English with "least proficient English speakers"); writes narratives as part of regional inquiry group.
2000–2001	Third-year teacher; collects data on conversation and communication patterns in her ELD class as part of school-wide inquiry. Joins CASTL program.
2001–2002	Fourth-year teacher; dismantles "English-only" rule in her ELD class; conducts collaborative research with fourth-fifth grade teacher; publicly presents the results of her inquiry to her colleagues and proposes to pilot ELD instruction with a heterogeneous group.

"I have a pit in my stomach and my mouth feels dry. *Where else do you speak English? How can I get you to speak more English? What is going to happen to you? What can I do to help you learn this language?* Janet is speaking Spanish to Valeria. Julie sits quietly next to Zenaida. George is speaking Spanish to Marisol. *Is anyone speaking English?"* (Capitelli, 2000).

For the most part, Capitelli's fear is relatively diffuse. She is not sure why her students are not speaking more English; she worries that it might be her own lack of experience or problems that the students have that are beyond her control, and she feels unprepared to respond.

Year Three (2000-2001)

Using Language to Make Sense of Text

By the summer between her third and fourth years, however, Capitelli begins to seriously examine her assumptions. She wonders whether the problems in her ELD class may stem from the "English-only" approach she has adopted, rather than the students' lack of skills or motivation or her own inexperience. In particular, she hypothesizes that her own actions and assumptions may be playing a role in limiting her students' participation in class and their use of English. As she put it in a written reflection in the summer of 2001:

> Am I asking them to talk for themselves in order to learn and make meaning, or am I asking them to talk for me? By connecting my reading to a number of elements of my practice (my English class, my report card comments, the "think-about-it" chair) I began to realize that I have created three norms of communicative behavior in the classroom: "too much" talking, "just right" talking, and "not enough" talking. These norms are very specific for particular settings in the classroom (the rug and student tables) that I have taken for granted as "good teaching" and that help me to maintain my authority and control in the classroom. (July 2001)

As she continues to examine her practice, Capitelli recognizes that she has been framing the problem in a way that denies one of her most basic beliefs about the power of conversation and discussion for learning:

> These norms are in direct conflict with how I believe that students learn (this isn't at all to suggest that communicative norms in a classroom should not exist). I know that students make meaning by using language with one another, but I am continually insisting that they stop talking when they are working in their journals. I know that learning English is not dependent entirely on speaking English, but when the students are speaking Spanish during the English hour I tell them to stop speaking Spanish and speak in English (the result of which is that they stop talking altogether). The reality is that I haven't been listening to what they are saying in Spanish during the English hour. My assumption is that if they are not speaking in English they are not learning English. But I don't know if indeed that is the case. I have simply been insisting that they participate in particular ways in particular settings. (July 2001)

Having come to this realization, Capitelli decides to make a major change in her instructional approach:

"I made a conscious decision in July [2001] to problematize the ways in which I had been using language in my own classroom. . . . Instead of language being a product that I was looking for—language could (and would?) be a vehicle. I dismantled my rule of no Spanish during English class." (January 2002)

Correspondingly, during this second phase of her development, Capitelli applies a strategy she has used successfully in her "regular" Spanish instruction—asking the students to use language to make sense of texts—during ELD hour:

> Instead of asking students to use language to talk about themselves in isolation, I have tried to use literature to create a common text among children that they can use. For example, the action of char-

acters, the dialog between characters, and the retelling and recreating of the story. I am also supporting students' use of primary language between one another in order to make sense of the content that we are covering. After the students have had the opportunity to talk with one another in Spanish, I have then been trying to create listening and speaking tasks in English. All of this feels like good teaching to me—it feels connected to my training and to theory. But within the context in which I am working it has felt impossible (until now) to teach this way. (January 2002)

Year Four (2001-2002)

ELD Instruction with a Mixed-Ability Group

As a result of what she is learning about her own practice, for her fourth year Capitelli decides to make a significant change in her ELD practice. Newly aware of some of the tacit assumptions about the use of English that are driving Manzanita's ELD program and her own practice, she decides to challenge herself "to think about language differently during ELD" and dismantles the rule of no Spanish during English class. She immediately notices a difference in both the students' activities and her own approach:

> First, English class is no longer quiet. There is now lots of talking and activity happening all of the time. Albeit most of it is in Spanish— but kids are talking to one another and talking about what we are doing in English class (content). Second, my own personal anxiety about my students and their success has dramatically lessened. I no longer find myself panicking about how my students are doing and my own failure as a teacher of English. My students are asking me questions (in Spanish) and I am answering those questions (in English)— we are having conversations during English class. Somehow that feels much more productive than what I have been doing in the past.

Hypotheses about other key constraints on her students' development quickly follow. In particular, her work with other teachers and her continuing examination of students' language use and growth in her class leads her to wonder about possible negative influences of the overall structure of the school's ELD program on students' learning. Her concerns about the ELD structure crystallize as a result of a collaboration with Louise Stankowski, a new fourth grade teacher (who had served as Capitelli's student teacher the previous year). During the fall of Capitelli's fourth year, they decide to share their students during the ELD hour, with Capitelli sending half of her first-second grade students to Stankowski's fourth grade classroom and Stankowski sending half of her students to Capitelli's classroom.

When Capitelli walks into Stankowski's classroom for the first time, she immediately notices that eight of the fourth graders—the same students who had prompted many of her concerns when they were in her classroom as first graders—are still struggling, unable to make the transition to full English instruction. Although she had an initial hunch in her first year that these students would not be prepared to make the transition, that hypothesis is not confirmed until she sees those same students three years later. As she describes it in a written reflection during her fourth year:

> I have very distinct memories of my first class. I remember thinking that certain students would never be ready to transition into English. I remember feeling horrible thinking it—but there was something in my gut that told me that certain students were always going to struggle with English. And now, four years later, these students are not transitioning, they are all in the lowest English class, and they have all been put in the same class together (tracked?). The school and I did many things that we thought would help to ensure their academic success (retention, reading recovery, after school program, reports, etc.) but we did nothing to change the structures in which these students were working. We didn't change the structure of the ELD class or ask what do we need to do differently—it was all based on what the students needed to do differently. Are there students in my class this year that I think won't be ready to transition into English (yes!) and can problematizing my teaching (and maybe the ELD structure) impact student achievement? (January 2002)

The recognition that a number of students are not making the transition even after the many interventions the school provided raises numerous questions for Capitelli and Stankowski about what happened to these students in second and third grade. To pursue these questions, as part of their school-wide inquiry project, Capitelli and Stankowski interview the second and third grade teachers about their perceptions of the development of these students. Subsequently, after sharing the findings from the inquiries, Capitelli proposes to keep her whole class for ELD instruction—effectively creating a more heterogeneous group. After considerable debate (and over the objections of the principal), during Capitelli's fifth year the school's site council allows Capitelli and one other teacher to embark on a pilot experiment in which they work with a heterogeneous group of students during ELD hour.

All in all, over this time, Capitelli's understanding of her ELD practice evolves from a general sense of frustration and powerlessness to specific hypotheses about the kinds of changes in classroom strategies and school-wide policies that can help to improve her instruction. Her learning reflects a gradual deepening of her understanding of her own beliefs and expectations, the character and needs of her students, the power of different pedagogical strategies, and the assumptions and effectiveness of the school's approach to ELD instruction. In turn, as Capitelli learns how to change her practice, she develops insights and artifacts that influence her peers and provide concrete representations that can travel beyond her own contacts and context.

Four Key Influences on Learning in Teaching

Prior Knowledge, Context, Social Interaction, and Representations

Studies from three different research traditions—research on cognitive development, sociocultural learning, and organizational development—suggest several key influences that need to be considered in explaining what Capitelli learned and how she did so: the

prior knowledge and experience that teachers bring into the classroom, the *interactions* they have, the *representations* of thinking and
practice that they develop and have access to, and the *contexts* that
shape their opportunities to draw on their prior knowledge, interact
with others, and develop and access representations (see Figure 3.1).[2]

Prior Knowledge and Experience

The Roots of Capitelli's Learning

The influence of Capitelli's teacher education coursework, her previous experiences in classrooms as both a student and teacher, and
the books and resources she has read all reflect the power and limits of prior knowledge. These sources equip her with a repertoire of
materials, strategies, and approaches from which she can draw in
the classroom; they cue her in to important events or problems in
her teaching; and they provide her with vocabulary and categories
to label and describe her experience (Grossman, Smagorinsky, &
Valencia, 1999; Markus & Zajonc, 1995; Wideen, Mayer-Smith, &
Moon, 1998).

Figure 3.1. Four Key Influences on Learning.

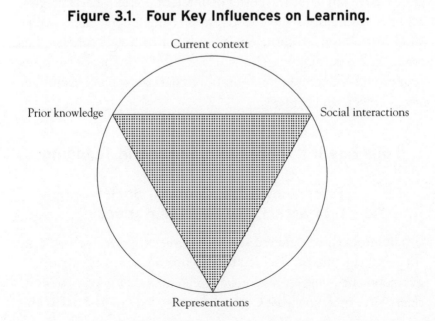

In particular, Capitelli's preservice preparation and her previous teaching experiences help her to recognize that something is not working in her ELD class, and they provide a basis for developing the skills and strategies she needs to improve her practice. Through her courses and an internship at the preschool, Capitelli is firmly convinced of the value of a constructivist approach to learning. She believes that students need to use and experience language in meaningful activities and to participate in constructing their own understandings. These strong beliefs contribute to the discomfort that she feels at Manzanita when she cannot get her low-performing students engaged in speaking and using English, and they contribute to her growing recognition—her hunch—that something is not right in her classroom.

In addition, in her teacher education program Capitelli has gained a sufficient grounding in these theories so that she can sustain her beliefs even in a context in which these theories do not initially seem to apply, and they help to propel her on her quest to understand her students' experiences more deeply. Finally, Capitelli's preparation encourages her to reflect on and inquire into her practice, and she begins to develop some of the inquiry skills she uses to explore her hunches and concerns at Manzanita. Beyond specific inquiry skills, Capitelli also learns about the work of a variety of teacher research groups that subsequently provide contexts that support her inquiries.

At the same time, consistent with numerous studies of learning in formal education settings (Wideen et al., 1998; Bransford, Brown, & Cocking, 2000), Capitelli finds that what she learns in other settings cannot be applied easily in her ELD instruction and that none of her previous experiences provide her with the kind of practical knowledge and information she needs to get her students to speak English. For the most part, neither her preservice coursework nor the textbooks and teaching materials that she is given by the district include the kind of practical direction and specific strategies she wants in order to design lessons that can engage her students in English language activities or to develop assessments that can help her understand why her students are so reluctant. For example, the

ELD textbook, teachers' guide, and standards for ELD classes given to all teachers in her district assume that all instruction is in English, not in students' primary language, as it is at Manzanita. Surprisingly, Capitelli also finds that there is little that she experiences in her own student teaching at Manzanita (which does not include work in an ability-grouped ELD program) that she can carry into her practice as an ELD teacher. Although the physical setting is the same as the one she experiences as a student teacher, the composition of the class in ELD hour (a group of the students experiencing the most difficulty) and the content (explicit instruction in English) are very different; as a consequence, Capitelli has great difficulty transferring anything she has learned as a student teacher to her work in the ELD class.

Space, Time, and the Organization of Activities

The Context for Teachers' Learning

The organizational context in which Capitelli works also has a profound impact on structuring and shaping her learning. Context dictates the people with whom Capitelli comes in contact and shapes their interactions; it influences the extent to which Capitelli can reflect on her practice; and it affects her ability and the ability of her peers to get access to representations of one another's practice (Solomon & Perkins, 1998; Bransford, Brown & Cocking, 2000; Greeno, 1997; Grossman et al., 1999).

Physical Layout. The physical layout of Manzanita structures access to the knowledge, ideas, and support that Capitelli can get from her peers. As is the case for many teachers, the geography of Capitelli's classroom, with two doorways—one into a busy hallway, the other into the room of another first-second grade teacher—and her busy teaching schedule mean that Capitelli spends most of her time working in her classroom, isolated from colleagues. She is only able to have daily, brief interactions with her next-door neighbor, and they catch only glimpses of each other's practices. At times they share students or plan lessons together. Occasionally other teachers, staff, or the principal stop in, but usually to discuss administrative matters (absent students, schedule changes, and the like). In fact, these interactions hardly ever focus on Capitelli's growing concerns about her students or what she learns about how to address those concerns. On the few occasions when her principal conducts formal observations and evaluations, very little time is spent discussing Capitelli's classroom practice. As a result, Capitelli's ability to learn in practice, in the context of her own classroom, with her colleagues is relatively limited.

At the same time, the isolation Capitelli experiences also supports her learning by allowing her to conduct her class and her own activities without substantial oversight. Capitelli has the flexibility to develop curricula and strategies that she feels respond to the problems she identifies. Although she does not feel she knows enough practical strategies to lead her students, she does not have to implement a prescribed curriculum, and she can try to develop an approach that reflects the ideas that she developed in her teacher education program. Similarly, no one prevents Capitelli from taking notes, making observations, or collecting data about her practice by insisting that she teach in a certain way or in a certain sequence.

The Organization of Activities and Interactions. Key influences on peer interactions at Manzanita—including the schedule, meeting structures, allocation of resources, assignment of responsibilities, and sanctioned activities—determine the kinds of support for learning that Capitelli experiences. For example, the fact that Manzanita makes teacher inquiry a part of the school's approach to professional development creates time and encouragement for Capitelli to conduct systematic inquiries on her own and in collaboration with others. This school-wide support for inquiry increases Capitelli's contact with colleagues, creates opportunities for them to share developing ideas, and enables Capitelli to see what her students do in other classroom settings. Just as collecting data in different contexts allows researchers to generalize across those contexts, Capitelli is able to use these opportunities to confirm and disconfirm her hunches and to begin to develop ideas about the general features of her practice that apply across different years, teachers, students, and situations.

Cultural Norms and Routines. In addition to the physical context and organizational structure, the beliefs, norms, rules, and routines that shape the organizational culture at Manzanita influence the way in which Capitelli inquires into her practice, interprets data, and interacts with others (Hanson, 2001; March, 1999). In particular, during her first two years at Manzanita, many of her colleagues and superiors at the school believe that their approach to ELD instruction is working—or at least that it is more effective than other options. As a consequence, Capitelli gets the impression that what she experiences in her classroom is "normal," and that she is already doing what she needs to be doing in order to help these students make the transition to English in fifth grade: no one is expecting her to make changes—or pressuring her to do so.

The cultural norms and routines at the school also make it difficult for Capitelli to raise and pursue some of the issues in her own practice that most concern her. As a new teacher, Capitelli is particularly cautious about how she presents her ideas and her work. She is concerned that her inquiries might reveal problems in her practice and raise questions about her abilities as a teacher. Furthermore, she feels she cannot raise her growing concerns about the school's approach to ELD instruction because she lacks the legitimacy of more experienced teachers on staff. Capitelli also feels that some colleagues regard her as a favorite of the principal, and she wants to avoid added attention in the context of school norms of egalitarinaism.

It is worth noting, however, that Capitelli's learning is not wholly defined by the organizational constraints within her school. Capitelli extends the contexts in which she learns beyond the confines of the space, time, and culture of Manzanita by participating in the regional teacher inquiry network and the CASTL program.

These "outside" activities give Capitelli more incentives, structures, and encouragement for examining her practice, and they link her to knowledge, people, and representations of practice available in a number of other contexts.

Representations and Social Interactions

As prior knowledge sets the stage for Capitelli's learning, and contextual factors shape the arenas in which her learning is carried out, social interactions and representations serve as vehicles through which her learning is expressed and exchanged.[3] On the one hand, interactions and the conversations that come with them have the advantage that they allow meanings to be negotiated, tacit knowledge to be shared, and new insights to be recognized; but what people say can be misunderstood and conversations can be easily forgotten. On the other hand, representations can give knowledge explicit and fixed forms. Through the process of "reification," interpretations and ideas are projected onto the world and "create points of focus around which the negotiation of meaning becomes organized" (Wenger, 1998, p. 58). Furthermore, representations can serve as "boundary objects"[4] that externalize ideas and experiences in forms that can reach into other settings. These representations make it easier to recognize and remember fleeting ideas and insights and to preserve their integrity as they are shared among people and applied in different contexts (Latour, 1986).

Together, social interactions and representations contribute to Capitelli's learning in three crucial ways. First, her interactions with others and her own efforts to represent her thoughts and experiences in the classroom provide the motivation, distance, and validation needed to turn her tacit hunches into explicit ideas. Second, interactions and representations make it possible for her to get new information and new perspectives that challenge, enhance, and amplify her emerging hypotheses. Finally, interactions and representations provide key means through which she can share insights and practices with her colleagues and influence them; in turn, she can see what happens when her developing insights and strategies are applied in the work of her colleagues and peers.

Recognizing Problems and Crystallizing Ideas: Making Tacit Knowledge Explicit.   In Capitelli's case, interactions and representations go hand in hand: producing written representations enables her to share with her colleagues ideas she had not been able to express in conversations, and, in turn, discussions with colleagues allow her to develop new ways of representing what goes on in her classroom. Initially, for Capitelli, sharing representations of practice and interacting with colleagues helps her both to articulate the problem she is facing and to confirm that it is a problem that needs to be examined. For the most part, despite the support for inquiry that Manzanita provides, the primary locus for these activities is outside the school in the regional teacher inquiry network that meets quarterly. For those meetings, Capitelli writes narratives about her experiences in her classroom and discusses them with a group of peers that includes Sally Jones, a third-fourth grade teacher who teaches in the regular (or "sheltered English") instructional program at Manzanita.

More than outlets for Capitelli's initial fears and frustrations, these narratives give Capitelli some of the distance she needs to turn the complexities of an overwhelming situation into a problem she can begin to address. As she explains it in an interview:

> A lot of times something will be happening, and I will be having my internal thoughts but I'll just really push them away so that I'll keep doing something even though I'm really feeling bad about what I'm doing because I'm frustrated or because I don't know what to do or whatever. I know what I find is that when I write about it at another point and I let myself write down what I was really feeling at the time and then that sort of enables me to say okay, I thought I was frustrated about this and there's no way that I can answer this question or tackle it. What I realize when I am writing is I actually don't know about this so maybe I am going to try and look at this little,

this smaller piece. It somehow makes it more manageable on some level. (February 2002)

Representing her ideas in a written form also allows her to articulate concerns and ideas that she could not verbalize in her interactions at school:

Something strikes me and I write it down and there's this way I think by writing it down I feel that I can illustrate the complexity and then I can sort of talk about it. But it's hard for me to have a conversation with someone and say, "Yeah, I am really struggling with my kids who aren't learning English" if they have no [text to look at]. . . . It's only if they have some sort of text to work off of that they can get it. "Oh, okay, I can kind of have a window into what's happening in that room." (February 2002)

Although articulating this kind of tacit knowledge is a key step for Capitelli, it is not sufficient; but by sharing her interpretations with others, she can get help in sorting through her impressions and validating her interpretations. For Capitelli, the opportunity to share her narratives and emerging ideas with Jones is crucial:

She [Jones] teaches in a sheltered class and I think she had a lot of concerns about her kids who were struggling and I had concerns about my kids who were struggling . . . and she would write narratives and I would read them and I would write them and she would read them and so there was this sort of . . . this support that "Yeah, I know that that happens." (February 2002)

Through these interactions and by reading one another's narratives, Jones and Capitelli can share concerns about their classes and their own performances that they are uncomfortable sharing at school. Once they do, they can see that the problems they face are not unique. These problems are not just their own; the problems extend beyond their own classroom contexts.

Interactions with the other CASTL scholars also help to sustain Capitelli's development when her doubts and concerns resurface. When she begins to wonder anew if her problem is "just" the problem of an inexperienced teacher—a problem that more experienced teachers have already figured out how to resolve—Capitelli's CASTL colleagues tell her that she is not alone. In particular, CASTL scholars with over thirty-five years of experience and who work with comparable student populations describe to Capitelli similar experiences in their own classrooms, and they introduce her to research and writings that deal with similar issues. Thus Capitelli finds that even experienced teachers and researchers recognize the importance of "her problems," and they have no pat answers. In the process, her CASTL colleagues validate Capitelli's articulation of the problem and confirm the value of her inquiry.

Gaining New Information and Perspectives. At the same time that interactions and developing representations help Capitelli to confirm interpretations and validate developing insights, they also create opportunities for her to get new information and knowledge that can challenge, extend, and amplify her learning. For Capitelli, conversations with her own students and instructional aide and examinations of her curriculum materials, her students' work, and the comments and reflections that represent what goes on in her classroom all play crucial roles in challenging her emerging insights about her ELD practice.

For example, in Capitelli's third year of teaching, as part of the school-wide inquiries under way at Manzanita and with the support and encouragement of her colleagues from a local inquiry network, Capitelli develops a survey and interview that asks eight questions about her students' use of English and Spanish and their participation in class. Instead of confirming her initial hunch that her students lack the motivations and skills to speak English and that she lacks the experience to motivate them, the students' and aide's responses lead Capitelli to question her assumptions:

"[O]ne of the things that came up [in the interviews] was that they all liked to read and write in English. And I had just assumed that they didn't because they couldn't." (May 2002)

Her interactions with her instructional aide and students provide Capitelli with both a moment of disequilibrium and a sudden concern that she has been wrong all along. At the same time, those interactions also enable her to recognize a new possibility: instead of trying to motivate the students to use English, perhaps she can build on and take advantage of instances in which they do enjoy using English and are successful. This new perspective gives Capitelli the hope that there is something she can do: she can learn more about her students' experiences and try to reframe the problem.

Capitelli's growing insights are reinforced by her reviews of a wide range of materials, including the data she gathers and the narratives she writes—formal records created explicitly to help her reflect on her practice—and her comments on each of the students and examples of the students' work—informal records she produces during the course of her third year of teaching. For example, between her third and fourth years of teaching, Capitelli spends some of the free time she has at the ten-day CASTL Summer Institute looking over her students' report cards and categorizing them. Through this process, Capitelli finds that her comments suggest that the girls are much less likely to talk than the boys. However, when she compares her perceptions with those of the students and the aide, she finds no such disparity. The converging data from different sources causes Capitelli to wonder whether she is applying different standards to the work and participation of the girls and the boys and leads her to think about the ways in which her own perceptions may be influencing her students' use of language in her class.

Her interactions with other Carnegie scholars also inform her emerging recognition of the "norms" of communicative behavior she has created in the class. In those interactions, her colleagues give Capitelli references to a number of relevant articles (some of which she had read originally in her teacher education program). These references make it clear to Capitelli that although Manzanita (and Capitelli) have embraced the "English-only" approach to ELD instruction, there is no definitive research that has proven that students can learn English more quickly if they speak English exclusively. These references, and the encouragement of her CASTL colleagues, help to crystallize Capitelli's doubts about her instructional approach and reinforce her interest in analyzing how her demand that students speak English may actually inhibit them from learning English. In the process, Capitelli begins to identify one of the key sources of the discomfort she has felt in her practice. In her preservice training, she developed a strong belief in enabling students to use their native language as a means of constructing their own understandings. Although she has vigorously pursued this belief in her Spanish instruction, she has almost completely repressed it in her "English-only" ELD instruction.

Ultimately, at the conclusion of the ten-day Summer Institute, Capitelli articulates her emerging understandings in a visual representation: a three-by-five-foot poster to be displayed as part of an exhibition of all of the CASTL scholars' work. Although some of Capitelli's colleagues create posters that consist largely of texts or sections of texts and pictures, Capitelli, who describes herself as a "visual thinker," strives to show in this spatial representation ideas she cannot express in a traditional text. In the end, Capitelli emerges with a poster that shows an overhead view of her classroom with her students working at tables. Rather than simply marking some as "talking"—as engaged in instruction and using English— Capitelli marks the students in two ways: in blue ink she represents her own assessment of their participation and in yellow ink, the students' own impressions of their participation. By tacking two pairs of tinted "3-D" glasses to the poster—a blue pair that shows the students' impressions and a red pair that show Capitelli's—she creates a representation that enables her colleagues to immediately see what she has struggled for three years to understand: that although she viewed the students as "not talking" and "not learning," many of those same students saw themselves as participating in and enjoying speaking English. The poster also serves as a concrete embodiment of what Capitelli has come to understand about her role in constructing the students' language use in her classroom: what she has been doing and what she has been thinking about the students may actually have been discouraging them from using English in ELD hour.[5] According to Capitelli, it is this "mind shift" that allows her to see her students and her role with them through a completely new lens, and it gives her the confidence and perspective to dismantle the "English-only" rule in ELD hour and try a different approach.

Extending Insights and Having an Influence: Applying Ideas Across Contexts. At the same time that interactions and the development of representations inform Capitelli's thinking, they also make it possible for her developing insights to have an influence on others. In turn, as others build on her ideas, Capitelli gets the chance to see how what she is learning in her own classroom applies in different contexts.

In particular, the collaboration with Stankowski—the teacher responsible for the "least proficient" ELD students at the fourth and fifth grade levels—confirms one of the initial hypotheses that motivates Capitelli's inquiry. Furthermore, by involving the second and third grade teachers in interviews, Capitelli and Stankowski not only gather needed data, but they also prompt their peers to reflect on the character and quality of ELD instruction in their own classes and lead those teachers to share their emerging questions with other colleagues.

Although interactions with colleagues contribute to Capitelli's emerging understanding and create avenues for her to share her ideas with others, the development of representations also help to make her insights concrete and memorable. In turn, those representations of her learning serve as boundary objects that can cross contexts and take on a life of their own, reaching people and audiences far beyond Capitelli's own classroom. For example, in the middle of her fourth year of teaching and in the midst of her joint investigation with Stankowski, Capitelli draws a picture to help her explain to her CASTL colleagues what she is learning. The picture shows three trains on different paths heading for the same destination: transition into English by the fourth grade, or biliteracy (as defined by Manzanita) (see Figure 3.2). Each of the trains represents a different group of students: the first group, representing the "most proficient" ELD students, moves directly to the destination; the second group, representing those with an average level of proficiency, travels a more circuitous route, and receives a variety of interventions, but eventually reaches the destination; but a third group, representing the "least proficient" students that Capitelli and Stankowski teach, experiences numerous obstacles and derailments and never reaches the destination.

Figure 3.2.   Capitelli's "Three Trains" Drawing.

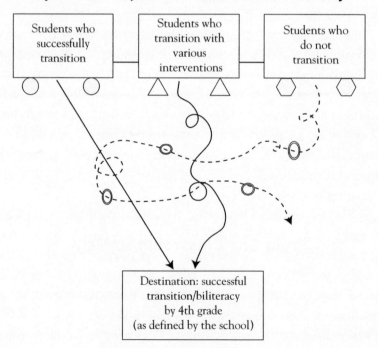

Capitelli's "three trains" representation is significant in several ways. First, it depicts students' experiences across grades and in different classroom settings at Manzanita. Second, it leads Capitelli and her colleagues to recognize that the school has created a de facto tracking system.[6] Third, the stark and concrete representation, and the subsequent discussions of it, give Capitelli the confidence that she has learned something valuable that she can share with others:

> Before, I knew [our ELD program] wasn't working, or I thought that I knew that it wasn't working, but I wasn't convinced enough to say it out loud. I could think it and I could feel it, but I wouldn't broach it. Because I didn't really have anything to say—"No really, it's not working." And I think now I do. And I have something to say—Yeah, I do, that's my thing. It's my own thing. It's not something that the state sends to us, it's not something that the district sent to us, it's not even something that [the principal] put in our boxes. It's the things that I did, what I looked at. (May 2002)

Finally, by creating a memorable representation that anyone can reproduce, Capitelli not only establishes "something to say," but she also puts it into a form so that others can easily pass on what they learn from her. In particular, this representation, which her colleagues can refer to simply as "the three trains," contains in those three words a complex set of ideas and perceptions related to the school's ELD approach. By compressing these ideas into memorable words and images, Capitelli gives her colleagues a shorthand, economical way to discuss and build on their experiences.

From One Classroom to Many

The representations that Capitelli develops and the widening circle of interactions in which those representations are discussed create a context that is prepared or "primed" to hear what Capitelli is learning. Like the "softening" of policy contexts (Kingdon, 1984),

Capitelli's colleagues are beginning to develop the language and background knowledge they need to comprehend the issues she is pursuing. Thus Capitelli's inquiry raises questions among her colleagues, influences her peers' investigations, and contributes to a developing school-wide conversation about when and how ELD students are making the transition to English, long before Capitelli draws the picture of the three trains.

At the same time that Capitelli's ideas and representations are filtering through conversations at Manzanita, her work is also beginning to make its way outside the school. Through her participation in the regional inquiry network and her interactions with CASTL colleagues, teachers from a number of different contexts begin wondering about bilingual instruction in their own schools and communities. Conversations with staff members at Carnegie lead them to share Capitelli's case and representations with research colleagues who have expertise in second language acquisition and bilingual instruction. As her inquiry develops, Capitelli also goes public with her investigation and shares her metaphors and graphics in formal presentations with a variety of audiences of teacher-researchers in the Bay Area and researchers at the annual conference of the American Educational Research Association.

There is no guarantee that Capitelli will be able to communicate her ideas in these venues in ways that will have a significant and demonstrable impact on others. But her experience with developing relationships and making presentations beyond her school context—which is not unusual for many teachers around the country, particularly those involved in formal inquiry and research projects—illustrates the many avenues through which teachers can influence a wide range of others even without producing published "peer-reviewed" research. Within her own setting, however, it is clear that Capitelli's ideas are having an influence when the school planning and management team gives permission to both Capitelli and another teacher to "untrack" their ELD classes. Furthermore, building on Capitelli's example, the management team makes plans to study these experiments and consider their implications for school-wide ELD instruction. If successful, Capitelli's experiment could serve as a model for changes to other ELD programs in the district.

Conclusion

Although the physical setting at Manzanita and the typical full teaching load constrain Capitelli's interactions with peers and limit her time for reflection, the freedom in the use of her time, the support for inquiries at Manzanita, and her connections to inquiring teachers outside Manzanita all help create opportunities for Capitelli to document and learn from her practice. These efforts to learn from her practice have not revealed the ideal set of pedagogies for teaching English to first and second graders, nor have they produced a clear picture of exactly how ELD courses should be structured. Her inquiry, the representations she has produced as a result, and her interactions with others have, however, allowed her to develop a deeper understanding of the relationship between her pedagogy and her students' English language acquisition. This has also resulted in a set of ideas and representations that have inspired her colleagues to make changes in their own practice and raised questions for a host of others involved in teaching, policy, and research. These representations are not packaged as a set of research findings. In fact, her depiction of students' paths through the ELD structure— in the drawing of three trains on different paths, the poster of her role in the patterns of discourse in her classroom, and the narratives she has written about her students—act as intermediate or draft representations that she has produced on the way to creating final products that she can submit for formal peer review, publish, or present.

In the process, Capitelli's experiences demonstrate what teachers can learn and how what they are learning can have a significant impact in improving policies and practices more widely. In particular, her case provides an illustration that a teacher's learning is not the simple musings of an individual absorbed with idiosyncratic concerns. Like her colleagues in the research community, Capitelli emerges with ideas and representations that have been vigorously reviewed and challenged: she has examined her assumptions, consulted existing research, taken advantage of other perspectives, tried out her ideas in different contexts, had her ideas and strategies replicated by others, and presented what she learned for public examination and critique. This may not be the same systematic process that some academic research goes through, but it is one that can yield ideas and information that can advance educational practice in numerous ways.

Questions for Consideration

When do teachers learn?

How do prior knowledge and contextual factors shape teachers' learning?

What roles can social interaction and the development of representations play in teachers' learning?

Notes

1. Manzanita has been involved in a number of reform efforts over the past ten years, including developing school-wide teacher inquiry projects, and has a reputation as one of the most effective schools in the most disadvantaged areas of a struggling urban district. The school has attempted to put those reforms in place while dealing with numerous problems and changes in leadership in the district administration and, most recently, severe budget cuts and a district-wide mandate to implement Open Court, a highly scripted reading curriculum. During this time, the school has been able to maintain its bilingual program only because numerous parents have signed waivers every year to exempt the school from the restrictions of the California state proposition limiting bilingual instruction. As part of their ef-

forts to improve instruction and in response to a growing concern among the school staff that English instruction for Spanish-speaking students was marginalized during the busy school day, the members of the school established the dedicated one hour of English instruction in 1997.

2. Studies of cognitive development often emphasize the internalization of abstract representations and the acquisition of knowledge and cognitive skills as products that can be applied across settings (Solomon & Perkins, 1998; Sfard, 1998). Studies that take a sociocultural perspective often focus on the sharing of tacit knowledge or "socialization" rather than viewing knowledge as a fixed entity or a product that individuals can acquire (for example, Wenger 1998; Lave & Wenger, 1991; Cole & Engestrom, 1993). Studies of organizational learning often address how knowledge is externalized so that it can be taken into account in training programs, decision making, and future planning (Hanson, 2001; Nonaka, 1994; Schön, 1983).

3. Social interaction and representation intertwine in professional learning to such an extent that it is almost impossible to talk about one without the other. Social interactions invariably involve the use and exchange of verbal representations and often other forms of text-based representations, and those representations themselves are inherently social and cultural constructions that grow out of interactions.

4. Boundary objects are "inscriptions that have mediating function, coordinate activities, and translate discourses of people from different communities" (Roth & McGinn, 1998, p. 36; see also Star & Griesemer, 1989).

5. The development of the poster further illustrates the interconnection between representations and interactions. In fact, in the CASTL Fellowship Program, Capitelli not only benefits from discussing her developing ideas with experienced teachers from around the country, she also has the opportunity to develop her poster while she works side by side with several

colleagues in shared office space. During that time, Capitelli experiments with different ways of representing which students were and were not talking in her class and asks for feedback from those around her, making adjustments as she goes. In addition, she can see the posters of her colleagues and can draw inspiration and ideas from them.

6. Similarly, researchers share ideas and influence one another's work by engaging in conversations, making informal and formal presentations, and circulating drafts of grant proposals, reflections, and research reports long before results are formally reviewed or published.

4

BEYOND THE SCHOOL

How Teachers' Learning
Can Advance the Field

Tim Boerst, Joan Cone, Renee Moore, and Emily Wolk demonstrate the kinds of contributions teachers can make to their profession that go far beyond the learning of their students. Boerst, a fifth grade teacher in what he refers to as an "urban suburban"[1] elementary school in Michigan, has helped to launch a Teacher Research Group (TRG) that engages teachers from across his district. Cone, a high school English teacher in a diverse suburban community in the San Francisco Bay Area, has played a leading role in abolishing tracking in English courses at her school and has carried out a variety of research projects that have contributed to both local and national discussions of detracking. Moore, a Mississippi Teacher of the Year and a Milken Teaching Award winner, speaks to a wide range of audiences even as she continues her work as a part-time high school English and journalism teacher and a "lead" teacher who assists with professional development. Wolk, a kindergarten teacher originally, works with colleagues in her school as a mentor and "resource teacher" in a large urban district outside Los Angeles.

The diversity of their experiences suggests that no single prototype defines what kinds of teachers can have an impact on others. These four teachers teach different subjects and different grade levels. They come from different parts of the country. Boerst and Wolk have been in the classroom for ten years or less; Moore has been teaching for over fifteen years and Cone for almost thirty years. Cone and Moore have garnered extensive national recognition for their work; Boerst and Wolk are known primarily within their own schools and districts. Wolk and Moore work in formal leadership positions outside the classroom; Boerst and Cone share their work and ideas with others while continuing to teach full-time. At the same time, as members of the second cohort of the CASTL program, all have documented their teaching in a number of different ways, and they have all had opportunities to learn how to inquire into their practice through some form of collaborative activity or guided instruction. Boerst's work with the TRG group began with his participation with a colleague in the certification process for the National Board. Moore learned about teacher inquiry when she participated in summer programs at the Breadloaf School of English; Cone learned how to look systematically at her practice when she became involved with a teacher research program through the Bay Area Writing Project; and Wolk examined her practice and developed her research skills when she went back to get her master's degree.

Looking across the range of their experiences suggests several other key commonalities in their abilities to impact others. In particular, in contrast to traditional leaders whose impact on others often relies on the power, authority, and control that can come with their formal positions in organizational hierarchies, the impact these teachers have comes from the expertise, credibility, and influence they bring to their activities, regardless of the formal positions they hold. Beyond a simple linear sequence—in which teachers gain expertise, develop credibility, and then start to have an influence on others—their experiences suggest that expertise, credibility, and influence are mutually reinforcing. These teachers build their expertise, credibility, and influence by engaging in personal and public inquiries into their teaching, deepening their understanding, and gaining the confidence that they have something worthwhile to say. They refine their insights in representations that give those insights a life of their own that can impact individuals and audiences they might never meet in person. The connections these teachers develop inside and outside their schools enable them to get new perspectives and shape their ideas for different audiences, and they give them access to individuals who can provide new ideas, information, and resources and serve as translators, advocates, and amplifiers for their work.

The Varieties of Influence

Although Wolk, Boerst, Moore, and Cone all make contributions to the advancement of ideas and improvement of practice and policy both inside and outside their schools, they represent at least three different kinds of contributions that teachers can make to the learning and development of other educators: Wolk's experiences illustrate the kinds of influence that teachers can have on the classroom practices of their peers, Boerst's activities demonstrate how teachers can have an impact on policies in their districts, and Cone and Moore's work highlights the state and national impact that teachers can have through their presentations and publications.

"Living Elbow to Elbow"

Support for Practice and Professional Life

As a resource teacher at a large elementary school in Santa Ana, California, Wolk has formal responsibility for helping her teaching colleagues to improve their classroom practice. But rather than using her authority to show or tell her colleagues what to do, she takes advantage of opportunities to work together with them. When people ask her to come into the classroom, she always tells them, "Listen, I'm not an expert. I only pretend to be." As she explains, "So if I work with somebody, I don't come and do this thing and walk away. I usually try to live with them elbow to elbow." Even when her colleagues invite her into their rooms to assist them, Wolk tries to transform the usual dynamic to subvert her role as "expert." "They are used to having someone come in and do a fancy lesson and give them a packet of stuff and then leave," she told us, but she tells her colleagues, "That is not who I am. That is not what I am about. Frankly, I am not an expert and maybe somebody else would be better at that, but what I provide is a colleague to bounce ideas off of."

In many instances, Wolk invites the teachers to watch her and help her deal with a problem she is having, only gradually moving to examine jointly the practice of her colleague. "I need your help, but I also will offer help," she told one colleague, and then invited the colleague to tape her doing a math lesson. "Okay, watch me," Wolk told her. "I'm telling you, this is going to be rough because I don't know your kids, I'm trying to figure them out and displaying myself." Wolk describes the process: "Then we watched her tapes. So she taped me first and then I talked through the conversation so she could see me doing it. God, that wasn't very pretty whatever was going on there. And then I said, 'Would you mind if I taped you?'"

Through these kinds of interactions, Wolk has helped a number of colleagues to deal with particular problems and issues with their practice. In one instance, Wolk worked with a relatively new teacher to help her engage her students in more productive discussions. In another instance, a veteran colleague told Wolk that she had run out of ideas for teaching reading and literature. They worked on lessons together, attended relevant trainings, and developed a new set of teaching strategies particularly suited to the needs of her weakest readers. In turn, these new strategies helped the veteran to regain her passion for teaching. "I think the thing that struck me the most," Wolk explained, "was that other people would say 'Wow, she is energized again!'"

As with this veteran, beyond her influence on classroom practice, Wolk's work helps to provide her colleagues with inspiration and support in other aspects of their lives. After Wolk received her National Board certification, thirteen other teachers at her school began the certification process (in the previous ten years only seven teachers in the entire district and none in her school had been certified). "I want to watch you first," a colleague told Wolk, and then, as Wolk put it, "they watched me go through it and struggle through it."

Like Wolk, Boerst, Cone, and Moore have all participated in groups or worked directly with other teachers to share and reflect on their practice. Their impact on peers in their local communities, however, extends beyond their schools. Many of them have led or participated in courses in local teacher education programs. Wolk herself has taught classes on classroom management and discipline and other issues through both Chatman University and the Orange County Department of Education; Boerst holds a position at the University of Michigan; and all four have organized or led groups in which they have helped other teachers to develop inquiries into their own practice.

"Oozing" Through the District

Creating More Responsive Policies

As Tim Boerst describes it, the ideas and activities of the Teacher Research Group that he helped to launch have "oozed" through the district.[2] Boerst and a colleague started the group primarily as a way of continuing the conversations with colleagues that they began when going through certification for the National Board for Professional Teaching Standards. However, as the group has evolved into a regular source of professional development for a number of teachers in the district, the district has steadily increased its support for the groups, and some district decisions and policies have begun to reflect the influence of the group's work and approach.

Although initially the district provided little more than a place to meet, in subsequent years they provided video cameras in all the schools so that the TRG members (and others) could tape their teaching. "We just gave them another reason to think about why those kinds of materials are useful," Boerst explained. "I think maybe their conception in the beginning was that those are useful for taping students when they do something. . . . But I don't think they had thought a whole lot about the use of videotaping in learning about teaching in professional development." The following year, the district provided funds to secure substitute teachers so that the teachers could observe in one another's classrooms, and the year after that the district provided release time for half-day meetings during the school day on a quarterly basis.

Hand in hand with the changes in their support for the TRG, the district also shifted their approach to district-wide professional development. When the TRG first began, the district was in the midst of developing a new approach to professional development that involved monthly "late-starts." Initially, however, the approach consisted of what Boerst referred to as a typical "potpourri" in which the teachers were briefly introduced to a variety of topics and issues over the course of a year. "Whatever was the hot button issue that we needed to worry about for that particular week, that's what the in-service training was," Boerst explained, and many of the members of the TRG were "vocal" in saying "this doesn't make sense, we're not learning anything." When Boerst and a colleague met with district administrators at the end of the year, they "talked about how that compared with what we were doing in-group and how we felt that group was helping us learn things about teaching, whereas these in-services, this hodgepodge of whatever, didn't seem to be doing the trick." The following year, however, as part of the implementation of a "Total Quality Management" approach, the district instituted a more practice-centered approach, with a full-year focus on *Understanding by Design* (Wiggins & McTighe, 1998). At the end of the year district administrators met with Boerst and members of the TRG again and asked specifically, "What are you learning from the teacher reflection group that would help us to think about late-starts?" In subsequent years, professional development activities during the late-starts have continued to reflect a year-long focus, and district administrators have continued to solicit the feedback of TRG members in refining their approach.

The work of the TRG has also served as a means of pushing the envelope on district policy in several other arenas. Once the group had established a process for drafting and completing narrative cases describing key issues in their practice, for example, they could show administrators a concrete and effective alternative to the conventional evaluation procedure. Boerst told us that TRG members felt that principals "should be able to read about our cases and know how we're thinking, that we've been rigorous about trying to improve something in our teaching. They can come and observe us based on that. They can look at our case and see that this is a nontrivial attempt to improve ourselves." Eventually, after reviewing the cases and seeing the work of the group, administrators in the district decided to accept the cases as a viable alternative to the usual district evaluation process. Today, as Boerst puts it, "We don't have to go through the whole district rigmarole."

In addition, Boerst is able to have a wider impact on policy and practice by taking advantage of new opportunities and pushing the district and the state to develop the ability to carry out new policies. "When I got National Board certification," Boerst explained, "one of the first things I had to do was reapply for my teaching certificate, like renew it. I have sixty credits of university credit that I could use to renew it, but I refuse to do it that way. And I made them [the state] take my National Board to do it, because they claimed that you could do that but they didn't know how to do it because nobody ever had them go through the paces to do it. So it's stuff like that . . . 'You say I should be able to [do that]—how are we going to make this happen?' It took three months to get them to figure out how to do it, but I did get a letter in the mail that they'd mass mailed to everybody who had National Board that said, 'Oh, you're now renewed.'"

As a member of a small district, Boerst has unusual opportunities to talk directly with his principal, the superintendent, and the assistant superintendents in order to influence their thinking and policies. However, even in larger, more bureaucratic schools and districts, Wolk has found ways to exert an influence on policy through the opportunities and responsibilities that derive from her formal positions and growing relationships with her "superiors." Renee Moore and Joan Cone, on the other hand, have had to be more overtly political, organizing teachers and others to advocate for a role for teachers in curriculum development, changing school structures (like tracking), and other aspects of school and district decision making.

Using the Teacher's Voice

Connecting Practice, Policy, and Research

When she began work on detracking, Joan Cone found herself drawn to the work of Jeannie Oakes and Glynda Hull, two researchers who have extensively studied issues of tracking and equity. "I wanted to be part of that . . . I identified with the people who inspired me from the writing. And I wanted to have my voice—my writing voice—join theirs."

Since that time, Cone has continued to share her research on tracking in a variety of venues—including *Newsday* (2002), *Harvard Educational Review* (1994), *College Board Review* (1993), *Phi Delta Kappan* (1992), and *Harvard Education Letter* (2003)—and she has presented her work at the annual meeting of the American Educational Research Association, in teacher education courses, and in public discussions. On one radio show, the breadth of Cone's influence was apparent when the moderator brought in a professor from the University of Virginia to respond to Cone's comments. The moderator described the professor as someone "who has actually been on the national side of this, the opposite of Joan Cone," but the professor corrected him, replying that she was a "great fan" of Cone and that she had "read and used" Cone's work for a "long time."

Beyond getting across specific information and ideas she has gained through her own teaching and research, however, in her writing and presentations Cone strives to demonstrate that teachers can be passionate and committed intellectuals with ideas and points of view that are worth paying attention to. In her view, more teachers should be out in public acting as "bridges" between research and practice, and more venues are needed in which teachers can have a real voice, not just a pat on the back. As she puts it, "I think lots of times that we go places they invite us—'Oh, let's hear from the teachers.' And they wine us and dine us and put us up in nice hotels and silence us." In response, she shares her writing, talks about the research she has read, and describes the political battles she has fought so that people "get used to knowing that teachers are political, we're thinkers, we're leaders, we're reformers."

As an award-winning teacher, Moore has had her share of "wining and dining." But the honors she has received have also expanded her audiences and extended her sphere of influence, so that she, like Cone, can share her experiences with a wide range of teachers and policymakers far beyond her own school in Shelby, Mississippi. In addition to invitations to speak at a variety of staff development sessions around Mississippi, Moore has been asked to speak at the state conferences of organizations such as the National Council of Teachers of English, the State Staff Development Council, and Future Educators of America.

In her writings and her presentations, Moore draws on her experiences as a high school English and journalism teacher and her own research on cultural engagement as a frame for what she has to say. At the same time, Moore has taken advantage of the opportunities that have come her way to make sure that audiences hear not only her voice but the voices of her colleagues. As she puts it, "There's this pattern, and I've seen it in a lot of places. You like to pat teachers on the back and say, 'Oh, isn't this wonderful. You do a good job. Here's your apple.' But you don't want to talk to me about the things that really matter—as if I have no professional opinion that's worth hearing when it comes to policy."

In response, Moore uses her research as an example of the fact that "teachers actually know more and do more than people in policy positions generally give us credit for," and, like a latter-day Johnny Appleseed, she gathers ideas and innovations in her visits to towns like Hot Coffee and spreads them across the state.

Although much of Boerst and Wolk's energy and influence is directed toward their peers and colleagues in their districts, they too participate in a variety of national venues in which they can communicate their ideas and those of their colleagues to a wider audience. Boerst serves as a chair and panel member of one of the review boards of "Teaching Children Mathematics," a journal associated with the National Council of Teachers of Mathematics, in which he has also published commentaries and articles (Boerst, 2003a, 2001; Boerst & Schielack, 2003). In addition, both Boerst and Wolk have presented at conferences like the American Educational Research Association (Wolk, 2004, 1998, 1997; Boerst, 2003b). Although it is difficult to judge the impact that Boerst, Wolk, Moore, and Cone may have in these venues, all serve as examples of the ways that teachers, even under current conditions, can extend their reach beyond their own classrooms and communities.

The Means of Making a Difference

The Growth of Expertise, Credibility, and Influence

What enables Wolk, Boerst, Moore, and Cone to influence others? Research on situated and organizational learning suggests that individuals' influence on the learning of their peers and the development of their organizations rests on the sharing of tacit knowledge in joint and parallel activities, the creation of explicit representations of knowledge that can be shared across contexts, the value or "warrant" of the representations and the individuals who produce them, and the receptiveness of the individuals and audiences who may benefit from the representations.

Like Carter, Hitomi, Hurley, and Capitelli, these four make tacit concerns and ideas explicit by reflecting on and examining their practice alone or with others (Nonaka, 1994). Developing representations that document what they learn from their reflections and examinations makes their experiences and insights available for others to examine and build upon. These representations—like Capitelli's narratives, poster, and "three trains" diagram (see Chapter Three)—act as "boundary objects" that can travel through time and space carrying their ideas to their peers as well as to policymakers they may never meet (Czarniawska & Sevon, 1996; Wenger, 1998). The extent to which their ideas "travel" through their schools and districts and influence others depends on the nature of their activities and representations, the connections they develop, and the norms, values, and culture in their schools. If these teachers were not perceived as having useful expertise, their colleagues probably would not have paid much attention to them, their inquiries, or the representations they produced. However, the fact that these teachers have managed to demonstrate their expertise both inside and outside the classroom helps to build their credibility and leads others to regard their inquiries and representations as "warranted" and worthy of examining, discussing, and sharing with others (Seely Brown & Duguid, 2002).[3]

Learning That Leads to Leadership

> Teacher research is not about looking for some
> great new way to teach: It is the prima ballerina at
> the bar; it is the concert pianist playing scales; it is
> the basketball star practicing lay-ups; it is digging
> for treasure deep in one's own backyard.
> —*Renee Moore*, Circles of Influence:
> Use of Dialogue Circles in Researching
> Culturally Engaged Instruction

Boerst, Cone, Moore, and Wolk have all been inquiring into their practice for a number of years. For each of them, those inquiries serve as a source of data, resources, and ideas that they can share with others. For the most part, these teachers begin these examinations in order to address their own questions and concerns. As was the case for Capitelli, their inquiries grow out of particular frustrations or moments of "disequilibrium" when they realize that things are going on that they do not quite understand. The distress or unease they feel in these situations brings critical issues to their attention. Rather than brushing these issues off, the teachers dive into them and seek to learn as much as possible about them.

The Sources of Lifelong Learning. "A frustrated outburst" in Renee Moore's teaching journal in her second year of teaching began her quest to understand why she was experiencing so much difficulty trying to teach Standard English to classes made up entirely of African-American students:

"I've only made it about halfway through the scoring [of a grammar diagnostic], but the results so far are depressing; most of the students' scores improved only slightly, several stayed the same, and some dropped! This is after a solid semester—two grading periods—of intense grammar instruction! So what now?" (Moore, 2005, p. 77).

"What now?" for Moore turned into extensive reading of literature on teaching English with African-American students, participation in a masters program and teachers' network through Breadloaf at Middlebury College, the collection of "boxes and bags" of data from her own classes, and continuing efforts to identify the elements of what Moore has come to call "culturally engaged teaching."

For Joan Cone, years of inquiry also began with frustrations and concerns about her practice. For Cone, participation in a graduate class that focused on the problems of tracking created considerable concern and anxiety as she began to examine her own efforts to work with low-achieving students in courses specifically designed to meet their needs, but in isolation from their more successful peers. In fact, before the graduate class, Cone had advocated for creating more tracks at her school in order to meet the needs of the lowest-performing students. "I wouldn't say anything in [the graduate] class." Cone told us. "People would all talk, 'Isn't it horrible these people track?' and I'd say, 'Yeah, a lot you guys know. You're not in these classes'. . . and I thought, 'Well, I'm teaching this class, and I'm a good teacher.' But the more I read, I really could feel a visceral change." After the class, Cone invited a faculty member to teach a version of the same course for her English department colleagues at her school, which launched their collective detracking efforts: "My thinking had really changed and so I didn't want to be by myself. There were other really caring teachers at my school. So I thought, they can learn what I learned."

Emily Wolk's inquiries were not always accompanied by the same sense of frustration as her colleagues, but they were fueled by moments of disequilibrium that brought critical issues to her attention. As Wolk put it, she felt "weird" when she realized there were some times when she couldn't go to the bathroom because the students were so engaged.

> [The students] would come early, they would stay late, they would be in there at lunch, they wanted to be in during recess. "No, teacher we're learning. We're doing this. We're doing that. Can you not go to the bathroom? Because that means that we're going to have to leave the classroom." . . . . There were other times where it was like you opened the door and they were out faster than lightning. "Goodbye." And I thought, "Wait a minute. What's going on here?"

Wolk's ensuing efforts to document what was happening in her classroom enable her to recognize that her students are most engaged when they are involved in "action-based" projects in which they pursue issues—like traffic safety—that matter in their community.

Engaging Colleagues and Reading the Literature: Situating Work in a Wider Context. Following such moments of disequilibrium, the teachers we studied embark on extended documentation efforts to conduct interviews, hold focus groups, collect student work, or develop reflections and cases to help them make sense of these issues. Wolk and Moore describe their inquiries as independent pursuits that they choose not to discuss with school colleagues, but all four teachers share their inquiries with other teachers and in teacher networks beyond their own schools. Cone regularly discusses her work and research as part of her involvement in the National Writing Project. Many of the issues and questions that Boerst pursues grow out of the Teacher Research Group that includes teachers from his school as well as others in the district. Wolk regularly examines her inquiries with colleagues in a local teacher education program where she was a student and now, at times, serves as an instructor. Moore participates in the Breadloaf Rural Teachers Network and has discussed her research with a network of lead teachers associated with the Southeast Regional Vision for Education (SERVE). These conversations and activities with peers inside and outside their schools provide the teachers with new perspectives, create opportunities for them to develop their inquiry skills, and give them access to critical resources and ideas they may not encounter on their own.

Gaining New Perspectives. The new perspectives and ideas that came from conversations with colleagues help these teachers to understand how their experiences relate to others. Thus, although they are all focused on addressing local issues of particular concern to their students and their school context, they pursue these issues with an eye to what is known and understood in other schools and in academic research. Finding that other teachers have similar issues and concerns helps to give the teachers confidence that they are not alone and that they are facing problems and issues that are not simply a function of their own inadequacies or limited skills. Talking with other teachers outside of her school and having others express interest in what she was doing helped Wolk to recognize that what she had to say might have relevance for other teachers. She was particularly struck when Joan Cone, whose work she had read prior to becoming a Carnegie scholar, mentioned reading Wolk's work. "I didn't know her—but she said she had read my work—read my work? Good Lord, what does that mean?—but it means I had something to say and she appreciated it."

With the recognition that they are facing problems that go beyond their own classrooms, they can then get new perspectives and ideas from teachers in different contexts. As Cone puts it, she wants to have somebody read her work and see if it "rings true." "It's just neat to have somebody say, 'No, that's not true. You better go back and think that over again.'" For Moore, the perspectives of colleagues from a different geographic region made all the difference. Moore explained that visitors to her school who lived in the North commented repeatedly "on the distinctive 'Southernness' of the school. They pointed out that her context was 'Southern' in the sense of the traditions of the African-American communities of the old rural South, which were evident throughout the school. For example, having teenage students call them 'ma'am,' and watching our parent volunteer hang elaborate Christmas decorations on each classroom door" (Moore, 2002, p. 4). By pointing out that these things were part of Moore's cultural context, Moore's colleagues encourage her to define carefully the different elements of culture that she has to take into account in order to develop her own model of "culturally engaged teaching."

Gaining Access to Resources. In addition to the specific ideas and feedback they get from others, colleagues also lend books and articles, point to relevant research, and provide introductions to ideas and people these teachers might not normally encounter. For example, the literature reviews that many of the teachers carry out often begin with references from their colleagues who help to steer them to useful articles and authors. For the most part, however, these teachers do not read the research literature simply to find strategies or approaches that they can implement in their classes. They read the research to gain information and ground their thinking; to check their assumptions and see if others have found similar problems or already found some answers. As Moore put it: "I was both thrilled and dismayed to find the questions I was raising had in fact been asked many times by an array of experts" (Moore, 2002, p. 6).

Most of the time, however, reading the literature does not solve their problems. Moore continued, "The review was helpful, but it was not enough to answer the questions my classroom situation presented. I found it difficult during class time or even after school trying to make connections between all the reading I had done of the academic research and what I was dealing with daily in the classroom. One important lesson I did take away from the research was that there was not any one particularly effective method of grammar instruction with Black students" (Moore, 2002, p. 5).

Rather than helping them resolve issues, talking with colleagues and reading the literature helps these teachers to frame their questions, inform their practice, and deepen their inquiries. In Moore's case, reading the literature allows her to see that no research adequately addresses the particular issues she faces, and it enables her to develop an approach to "culturally engaged instruction" that reflects the geographic and cultural context in which she teaches.

By working with colleagues and reading the literature, teachers like these begin to recognize the intellectual history of their work and ideas. They can see the problems they are addressing and what they are learning as connected and contributing to ongoing lines of work and inquiry pursued by others in both research and practice. "I now know who has influenced me," Cone explains, "and I can almost stand outside and look at my thinking." Although these teachers are developing ideas and information firmly grounded in their local practice, "expanding their circle" (as Moore describes it) allows them to place that local experience in a much wider context.

Representing Learning

Articulating and Sharing Lessons from Practice

Although the moments of frustration and disequilibrium that prompt their inquiries could have passed undocumented, in many cases Boerst, Cone, Moore, and Wolk capture these moments in journals, conversations with peers, or audio or videotapes that make their experiences hard to ignore and easy to remember. By collecting data, recording their impressions, and reflecting on their experiences, these teachers develop representations that help them to articulate what they are learning. Representations crystallize thinking by clarifying insights in tangible and memorable forms, and the drafting and revision of representations can produce a depth of understanding that makes it possible for the teachers to communicate and apply their ideas in different contexts.

The teachers' efforts to represent their practice encompass both the process of developing labels, categories, graphics, and other forms that capture particular ideas and observations and the creation of cases, articles, presentations, and other products that organize and present the results of their inquiries. Although all four of the teachers we studied rely on linguistic representations to develop their ideas, several also take advantage of charts, illustrations, graphs, and other spatial forms to help crystallize their ideas; as part of their CASTL projects, all four have also explored the use of multimedia to document their classroom experiences and to convey their experiences and ideas to others.

Using Language to Articulate Experience and Represent Classroom Practice. All four of the teachers we studied take advantage of both informal and formal opportunities to share their work with others to develop and get feedback on their representations of their practice. For example, Boerst and the members of his TRG regularly share their emerging ideas in their meetings, and they articulate what they are learning in meetings with administrators and other teachers "in the hallway." These informal occasions to go public allow them to test out what they are thinking, to see if they can explain their ideas clearly, and to develop new terms and representations to advance and share their ideas.

Through their discussions, for example, the members of the TRG developed and refined the language they use to discuss the way they teach writing. As they reviewed the writing process used in different classes, they recognized that many teachers used the term *revising and editing* as if it were a single step in the writing process. Subsequently they developed cases that examined whether students were able to distinguish between revising (substantially rewriting or reorganizing their work) and editing (making corrections in grammar and spelling). Based on what they found, the teachers who produced the cases—as well as many of their other colleagues in the group—have changed the way they talk about and teach writing by making a clear distinction between revising and editing—and teaching each one in a separate lesson.

For her part, Cone believes that "it's only in writing" that she begins to "work things out." As a long-time member of the Bay Area Writing Project and author of a number of articles, it is not surprising that Cone thinks of herself as a writer. But the writing goes hand in hand with the development of concepts, terms, and language that she can use whether she is writing an article, talking with a group, or simply reflecting on her own. Cone (2003) described the evolution of her use of the term *co-construction* in a study of a "difficult class" that she eventually titled "The Co-construction of Low Achievement" (later retitled "The Construction of Low Achievement").

> The idea was floating in my head. But I think it was only when— and it's been floating around in my head for a long time, so I've been aware of how students are constructed—but only when I did that piece of research on the co-construction, and gave it a name, that was really helpful to me, to give it a name. And I didn't have a name for it until last summer I think. When I gave it a name that helped me a great deal. But it was only in studying that one class and [seeing] what a low work ethic they had and all the shenanigans that they would pull so they didn't have to do any work that I began to see, "Yeah, they are actively participating in this."

Similarly, Moore develops metaphors that allow her to convey the complexity of culturally engaged teaching in succinct ways. Thus she compares her approach to teaching to the "jam sessions" and improvisations of jazz. Far from being on-the-spot invention, she argues that her ability to improvise in the classroom and respond to and build on the strengths and backgrounds of her students reflects years of practice and the ability to draw on a host of themes and instructional strategies when opportunities arise. In turn, her colleagues can take the jazz metaphor and apply it to their own teaching or share it with others.

Beyond Writing: Searching for Different Means to Represent Practice. All four of the teachers rely on writing in some way to help them examine and articulate their experiences in the classroom. Cone writes articles; Moore writes in her journal; Wolk produces classroom narratives; and Boerst drafts cases that focus on one aspect of his practice over the course of a year. But like many of their CASTL colleagues, these teachers also experiment with different modes of representation that can provide different perspectives on their practice that can lead to unexpected developments and outcomes.

Despite the importance that Cone ascribes to writing, the many other acts of representation entailed in the collection and analysis of data are also crucial in helping Cone to articulate what is going on in her classroom. For example, in order get a better understanding of the relationship between the previous high school courses her students had taken and their performance in her "untracked" advanced senior English class, Cone produced a chart. The chart compared the courses taken in ninth and tenth grade by the highest and lowest achieving students in her twelfth grade class. When Cone looked at the chart, in what she described as a "chilling" moment, she quickly recognized what she had long suspected. The school's course assignments and the students' own course selections resulted in a clear pattern. Even though all of these students had participated in untracked English classes as freshmen, the highest-achieving students enrolled in large numbers of advanced courses in other subjects, whereas the schedules of her lowest achievers revealed a preponderance of electives and low-level courses. From Cone's perspective, what was particularly shocking was not that the lowest-achieving students in her English class were also in lower-level math and science courses; what she had not realized until she looked at the chart was that many of these students were also actively choosing (and were allowed to choose) to take frivolous electives (including serving as teaching assistants who make copies and perform other minor administrative duties) and low-level courses in no sensible sequence. Cone was immediately able to take that chart and share it with other colleagues to help make her argument that the school—and the teachers themselves—were "co-constructing" low achievement with the students by allowing them—and in some cases encouraging them—to take unproductive courses.

For Boerst, the need to select video clips of his work in the classroom for discussion in the Teacher Research Group led him to rethink his assumptions about when students were and were not engaged in his work. In one instance, he watched as he effectively ignored and shut down what he assumed to be a student's distracting behavior, only to recognize that the student was engaged in pursuing a series of questions that could have led to valuable learning. That episode, unseen until captured and reviewed on videotape, helped to launch Boerst's expanding inquiry into student ownership.

In part, audiences find the work and representations of these four teachers credible and valuable because they are grounded in real practice and presented in forms that others can understand. In addition, however, like Boerst's videos—which are sometimes painful to watch—the representations that these teachers develop capture both the strengths and the weaknesses, the successes and failures in their practice. Cone has over thirty-five years of experience in the classroom, yet her work on the co-construction of low achievement focuses directly on some of the ways that she contributed to problematic student behaviors like the failure to complete assignments and attend classes. Such realistic portrayals often resonate with the experiences of others and lend credibility to these teachers' representations.

Making Connections and Building Networks of Influence

Despite the isolation that many teachers feel, Boerst, Cone, Moore, and Wolk have forged numerous connections with people inside and outside their schools. In part, their ability to develop "something to say" and to shape their representations to fit the demands of different audiences helps to build those connections. These connections then provide them with further opportunities to share their ideas and reach larger audiences. In turn, their growing network of connections gives them access to more resources and expertise that they can bring back to their schools and share with others.

Connections Make Connections.   In Joan Cone's words, researching and writing gets teachers' voices "out there and so they begin to have contacts that other teachers don't have." In her own experience, when she began to write, "people began to hear about me," and she began to get requests for speaking engagements and articles. Those contacts, in turn, led to more writing and speaking opportunities and a rapidly growing network of connections. The connections of the teachers we studied are also facilitated by the fact that many are involved in established networks through which their work and news of their work can travel. Thus, by participating in the activities of the National Writing Project and the Breadloaf Rural Teachers Network, teachers from around the country can hear about the work of Cone and Moore. These connections, in turn, give these teachers a set of colleagues ready to respond to their work, as well as associated presentation and publication opportunities to encourage them to share their work with others. In essence, these affiliations help to provide some of the institutional infrastructure and incentives and the community support that facilitate the research and scholarly work of researchers who work in university settings.

In addition to giving the teachers access to other opportunities, audiences, and resources, involvement with these kinds of national networks and organizations can also help to justify and legitimize their activities. In the eyes of district administrators, Boerst's TRG group gains credibility because it grew out of the teachers' efforts to support one another through the National Board certification process. By affiliating their work with the National Board and raising the possibility that more district teachers will attain that distinction, the TRG seems less idiosyncratic and more justifiable as part of a nationally recognized and valued enterprise.

Although some of the connections teachers make primarily give them access to other people and audiences for their work, some individuals and organizations act as bridges, amplifiers, translators, and advocates who can extend the value and influence of the teachers' contributions. For Moore, SERVE not only provides her with opportunities to meet with Teachers of the Year from other states in the Southeast, it also publishes and publicizes the results of the proceedings and creates opportunities for her to meet with groups of administrators and policymakers. Furthermore, like a referral from a friend or a trusted colleague, SERVE's endorsement gives Moore both visibility and credibility with audiences and individuals who might not otherwise pay much attention to her. Organizations like SERVE also can extend and refine the messages and ideas that Moore and colleagues develop. As Moore explains it, "Through SERVE, those of us who are Teachers of the Year have a chance to impact policymakers because they listen to SERVE. They don't necessarily listen to us, but they listen to SERVE. And because SERVE listens to us, they'll take our idea sort of second-hand." In the process, organizations like SERVE can draw on their own expertise and connections to translate the input from teachers into forms (such as policy briefs and briefings) that fit the demands of different audiences. As a consequence, the work of influencing others is not left entirely up to these teachers themselves; the work of influencing others is distributed and shared with key individuals and organizations.

Trying to Stay Connected: Working Against Status and Position. "Going public" with their work and building these kinds of connections brings numerous benefits to these teachers; nonetheless, the notoriety, status, and rewards they may gain also can create perceived and real inequities and alienate them from school colleagues who also work hard in the classroom or see themselves as equally deserving of recognition and reward. As a result, all four teachers actively pursue a variety of strategies to downplay their accomplishments and, essentially, to maintain the diminished status common to most teachers. These teachers work to maintain their relationships and credibility with other teachers by making themselves open and vulnerable to examination and critique by others. For example, when Cone gives workshops and makes presentations, she insists she is not "an outside expert" or "another little act" who has all the answers. Instead, she presents herself as a researcher who has been studying particular issues or making particular observations about her students. As she puts it when she makes presentations, "I am somebody who is thinking about the same things you are thinking about." In this manner, Cone and the other teachers present their experiences and invite others to explore the implications, rather than assuming that their strategies or approaches can or should be replicated.

Even in instances in which these teachers could have formal authority over other teachers, they often choose to rely on the credibility that comes from their shared experience in order to have an influence. In fact, in their roles as lead teachers, Moore and Wolk frequently "work against position" to undercut the authority that might give artificial weight or power to what they say and write. Although Wolk has the authority to critique the practice of other teachers, she often invites colleagues to watch her and help her deal with a problem she is having, only gradually moving to examine jointly the practice of her colleagues. As a lead teacher, Moore has a similar position of authority at her own school, and she helps to plan, coordinate, and carry out a variety of initiatives. Furthermore, with all of her teaching awards, Moore stands out among her colleagues. Yet Moore rarely talks about her research at her school. "I have to be very careful," she explained, "because I worked very hard to develop this working relationship with my faculty and if I talk too much about my own work, then that is taken as bragging. That is part of the culture of our community." Similarly, Moore demonstrates her concern for her credibility with her colleagues by redesigning her position and turning it into one to which teachers had to be elected by their peers. That means that in order to keep her position (and the increased salary associated with it), Moore has to apply for the job, like any other teacher in the district:

> So I essentially gave up my position as lead teacher and reapplied to become a part of the teacher leadership program. And they thought I was crazy. My principal told me I was crazy, she'd tell it to my face: "You're nuts. You're going to take a cut in pay and you're going to reapply? What if they decide not to give it to you?" just out of meanness or something like that. I said, "That's not the point. I think I should walk into the room just like everybody else that wants to be part of the [committee], lay my credentials on the table, explain why I deserve to be on this committee.

In this manner, Moore, like Wolk, refuses to bank on the power and authority that could come with her formal position, and chooses instead to align herself with other classroom teachers. In the end, the gamble pays off as her colleagues elect her to the position.

Tightening the Connections: Getting Ideas Out and Bringing Resources and Expertise "Home."   At the same time that key individuals and organizations enhance the influence of the teachers we studied, the teachers themselves can act as "bridges" between their colleagues and individuals and organizations outside their schools. Because of the connections they have built, the credibility they have established, and the expertise they have gained in getting ideas across to different audiences, they can amplify and translate the ideas of their colleagues, reach appropriate audiences, and bring back ideas and resources that benefit their colleagues. Both activities help them to demonstrate their value and their credibility, which, in turn, can help to deepen their relationships with colleagues and reduce the problems that any real or perceived inequities may cause.

Boerst, for example, meets with district administrators on a yearly basis, but those discussions focus on the work of the TRG, not on his own research. In the process he can share ideas and perspectives from other group members with the administrators and gain valuable information about policies, resources, and future directions for the district that he can bring back to share with his peers. Thanks to his work with the journal *Teaching Children Mathematics*, Boerst can also act as a "translator" by providing feedback that will help teachers who submit manuscripts to meet the demands of reviewers. By serving as an editor for a new department— "From the classroom"—that he helped to create, Boerst also works as an advocate for teacher research, and he can facilitate the publication process for teachers who write about their knowledge of mathematics instruction.

Similarly, when Moore meets with administrators, policymakers, and others, she sees it as part of her responsibility to make sure that the voices of teachers get "out there." As a result, she spends at least as much time in her meetings talking about the work of other teachers and championing the importance of listening to teachers in general as she spends discussing her own research. In particular, Moore has engaged in numerous discussions in her own district to persuade administrators to give the teachers more control over curriculum, professional development, and other issues. "I'm leveraging my awards and stuff as much as possible in this argument," Moore told us. "I said, 'Look; within a year's time I have received every possible recognition that you can get that says I'm some kind of decent teacher. I passed my National Boards. I won Teacher of the Year. You gave me another contract. I must be some good at what I do.' But it's hard to fight this fight. They'll acknowledge the fact that you're a good teacher in the classroom with your students. But they're hard-pressed to take that to the next level and say therefore, you must really know about education."

Moore also tries to reinforce her arguments about the value of teachers' experiences and expertise by drawing on the work of other teachers whom she has met through CASTL, Breadloaf, SERVE, and other connections she has established:

I love gathering information from one place and then spreading it in another. So when I do speak with teachers, a lot of times I'm bringing information about what's going on in other places that I've been in to them. . . . I very often mention my colleagues from Breadloaf, Breadnet, and things that I know they're doing. I talk about other schools I visited in the state. I like to do that kind of cross fertilizing because it's important, I think, for teachers to get that information across the boundaries of—you're not the only one who's going through this. You're not the only one—there's success [in other places], and other people are having the problems you're having. It's important to share that kind of stuff, and for a lot of teachers they don't hear that often enough.

Beyond simply sharing information, Moore also brings information and ideas home to her own district and tries to put them to work. She drew on what she learned about another district's approach to professional development, for example, in order to inform and argue for the changes in the teacher leadership program that she and her colleagues were eventually able to institute.

In addition to bringing ideas and information back to their colleagues, the connections that the teachers we studied had established also provided them with allies that they could call upon when they and their colleagues needed them. Cone, in particular, has established connections with a number of the most well-known local and national experts on tracking and related issues. These connections enable her to marshal evidence and resources to help launch and maintain detracking efforts in her high school. When administrators or other groups have questioned the value of detracking, for example, she can call researchers like Jeannie Oakes, Pedro Noguera, and Rhona Weinstein who respond with references and resources she can use to support her claims. In one instance, Oakes provided Cone with information about instruction for gifted and talented students that Cone used to demonstrate that their detracked English classes could meet these students' needs. Furthermore, as Cone has visited the classes of Weinstein, Noguera, and others at UC Berkeley, they, in turn, have been willing to "come right down" to the school to speak directly to the school board or others on behalf of Cone and her colleagues. As a consequence, all of these connections, many of which grow out of these teachers' initial inquiries, expand their influence outside their schools while helping them to support the work of their closest colleagues as well.

Conclusion

Conventional approaches to teacher leadership that focus on putting teachers in positions of authority imply that teachers' primary influence is on other teachers with whom they come in direct contact and those over whom they have some responsibility. In contrast, Boerst, Cone, Moore, and Wolk provide demonstration cases of the ways in which teachers can influence people they know well, as well as individuals they may never meet, whether or not they occupy formal leadership positions. In this view, teachers like Cone can have an influence on research audiences through their own articles and the citations and advocacy of researchers who become knowledgeable about their work; Moore and Boerst can have an impact on state and district policymakers by meeting with administrators and translating their ideas and those of their colleagues into terms familiar to those audiences; and Wolk can share her work and ideas with peers, teacher educators, and researchers who can help her to find new settings in which she can display, present, or publish what she's learning.

Although these four teachers, like many of their CASTL colleagues, have had an impact on a variety of different audiences, for the most part their primary motivation was not to exercise leadership and influence others, nor have they systematically endeavored to build and increase their impact. Rather, their impact on others has its roots in their research and scholarship. It grows out of their efforts to think deeply about questions and problems in their practice, to articulate what they are learning for themselves and for others, and to build and maintain their credibility with and connections to their colleagues. As they share ideas with others outside their schools, they gain a better understanding of what is and is not working in their schools, and they develop credibility as people who are willing to make public both the struggles and the successes in their practice.

At the same time, Boerst, Cone, Moore, and Wolk—like Carter, Hitomi, Hurley, and Capitelli—carry out their inquiries and make an impact on others in spite of the conditions in their schools, the criteria used to judge most research, and the norms and values associated with teachers and their activities. In order to have a positive impact on their students and an influence on their peers, policies, and the profession as whole, these teachers embrace the contradictions of learning and leadership. They engage in work that is both intensely personal and widely public, they ground their ideas in the specifics of their local situations while striving to make more general connections across contexts, and they demonstrate both confidence in the value of their experiences and humility in sharing those experiences with others.

Questions for Consideration

How can teachers have a positive impact on their peers? On their profession?

To what extent do teachers have to be "leaders" to have an influence on others? What does "intellectual leadership" look like?

What roles do research, representations, and social interactions play in expanding teachers' influence?

Notes

1. Boerst explained his use of the term "urban suburb," stating, "I would call where I teach an urban suburb. What I mean by this is that the district is in the very inner ring of 'old' suburbs of Detroit. You cross one road to go from Detroit to being in the dis-

trict, but there are few differences between one side of that road and the other as far as development/housing/populations (the two have been growing more similar as the years have passed)."

2. Boerst attributes this term to Judith Warren Little's descriptions of the ways in which professional learning in one setting has a tendency to creep into the many other settings in which teachers participate.

3. The value of the representations the teachers in this study produce may reflect what Eisner (1998) refers to as referential adequacy or the ability to provide guidance in making sense of experience: "If the guide is useful, we are likely to experience what we otherwise might have missed, and we may understand more than we would have without benefit of the guide. The good guide deepens and broadens our experience and helps us understand what we are looking at" (p. 59).

5

KNOWLEDGE OUT OF PRACTICE

Using Technology to Build
on Teachers' Expertise

Like her CASTL colleagues, Yvonne Divans Hutchinson has an impact on her peers and her profession. She serves as one of a number of teachers that Mike Rose writes about in *Possible Lives: The Promise of Public Education in America* (1996)—a book that describes the kinds of powerful and inspiring teaching that can be found in public school classrooms around the country. What's more, Hutchinson received her certification from the National Board for Professional Teaching Standards, and she has taught teacher education classes and spoken at numerous conferences and professional development workshops at her school and in her district. Even under these circumstances, it can be hard to get in-depth information on Hutchinson's teaching unless you meet her or hear her speak, and only a small number of people—like Rose or the assessors for National Board certification—have had much chance to actually see her teach.

The development of the Internet and other new technologies, however, has made it possible to imagine entirely new means of making teaching public and, in the process, to amplify and expand the influence of teachers like Hutchinson. For example, as part of her participation in the CASTL Program, Hutchinson worked with Desiree Pointer Mace and members of the Carnegie Knowledge Media Lab to develop a website (www.goingpublicwithteaching .org/yhutchinson/) that presents a rich array of materials to represent one day of teaching in her classroom.

Hutchinson's website is specifically designed to explore aspects of classroom practice that many teachers struggle with, including how to support the development of students' abilities to analyze literary texts and how to orchestrate classroom discussions that involve all students. During the single two-hour class session on which the website focuses, Hutchinson orchestrates a group discussion of some of the key issues in A Call to Assembly, an autobiography by the jazz musician and educator Willie Ruff. She uses this session and discussion to engage students in what she calls "thinking with text"— "the invisible 'beneath the surface' reading that requires interpretation and analysis" (Hutchinson, 2005, p. 185)—to explore the use of racially charged language and the relevance of literature for the students' own lives.

Rather than a linear lesson plan that dictates what teachers should do to replicate a single activity, the website provides a variety of descriptions of classroom strategies, including an "anticipation guide" to support students' reading and a list of "stock phrases" that can be used to help get students talking. Visitors can also spend considerably more time on their own or working with others to explore Hutchinson's approach by looking at short video clips that illustrate how the class and discussion unfolds, considering examples of Hutchinson's students' work, and scanning (online or on DVDs) the entire two-hour class session or a one-hour videotaped interview in which Hutchinson reflects on her work.

Beyond the class that serves as a focus of the site, the inclusion of Hutchinson's reflections on her own practice, additional video clips and curriculum materials showing what she does at the beginning of the year, and videos of the same students' projects and presentations the following year, allows viewers to get a glimpse of many other aspects of teaching and learning, including how Hutchinson creates a productive classroom climate and how her students' understanding and oral presentation skills develop.

Similar websites that capture the work of a number of other CASTL teachers include those that represent Renee Moore's work on teaching grammar in high school English in Mississippi, Joan

Cone's work teaching AP English to heterogeneous groups of students in Northern California, Emily Wolk's efforts to engage elementary students in community-based inquiry projects in Southern California, and Sarah Capitelli's work on English language instruction in her bilingual elementary class in the San Francisco Bay Area.[1]

One can imagine, in the near future, building on these models and others like them to create an online collection with fifty, one hundred, or more examples that show teaching and learning in a wide range of disciplines (mathematics, English, history, the arts, biology, chemistry, and so on), at different levels from early childhood through college. With a focus on developing sites that provide a small but rich set of materials, this collection could continue to grow each year to reflect the latest innovations and advances in teaching in communities around the country. Documenting teaching with students from a wide range of cultural backgrounds can help to discern and demonstrate the kinds of high-quality teaching practices that all students should have an opportunity to experience. As such, development of an online collection of teaching and learning could help to shatter the myth that powerful teaching depends on the heroic efforts of individual teachers, and it could demonstrate that high-quality teaching can take place in many forms, in many contexts, with all kinds of students.

Could an online collection of teaching and learning be established? Technically, the answer is yes. Many teachers already have their teaching materials and student work in electronic form and the technology exists to put papers, photographs, and other materials online; and new generations of faculty are growing up in an era in which activities like creating web pages and surfing the World Wide Web are as commonplace as playing video games and changing TV channels. But it takes much more than technology to document teaching and represent it in ways that will make it easily accessible to a wide audience (Hatch, Bass, Iiyoshi, & Pointer Mace, 2004). The experiences of those involved in the CASTL program and the issues detailed throughout this book point to three critical developments that are needed to use technology to make teaching public and to fuel significant improvements in preparation and practice: new forms of web-based representations; educational experiences that take advantage of those representations; and on-line forums for the discussion, interpretation, and critique of those representations. These developments can make it easier for large numbers of teachers to document their practice and to share their learning in ways that advance the work of their peers in general and that of new generations of teachers in particular.

New Forms of Representation: Capturing Expertise for the Future

For years educators have relied on static texts—such as lesson plans, textbooks, case studies, and research articles—to capture and convey what should be done in the classroom. Now multimedia and new technologies can facilitate the creation of sophisticated and innovative representations of teachers' instructional strategies and expertise. web-based multimedia representations of practice may be particularly useful because they offer viewers the opportunity to see and explore many different aspects of teaching and learning—including the complexity, richness, and emotionality of teaching—that are not easily observed in conventional representations (Pointer Mace, Hatch, & Iiyoshi, in press). They can also help viewers to develop an understanding of the complexities of teaching by allowing viewers to revisit the same material at different times, for different purposes, and from different perspectives (Spiro, Feltovich, & Coulson, 1992). Conceivably, the Internet may also enable viewers to get easy and immediate access to current representations of practice with many different students in a wide range of settings. Ideally, developing large numbers of these web-based representations will address the concern that new teachers and others often feel: that few cases or other examples of teaching that they encounter in their preparation and professional development experiences reflect the realities of their own classrooms.

Although new media and the Internet offer possibilities for capturing the complexity of teaching in ways that traditional texts cannot (Hiebert, Gallimore, & Stigler, 2002), they also come with their own constraints that affect their usefulness. In particular, viewers may find it hard to interpret and understand the work of teachers like Hutchinson unless they have sufficient background knowledge about teaching and the contexts in which the teaching takes place, as well as some experience in navigating and "reading" websites and unconventional forms of representation (Bransford, Brown, & Cocking, 2000). The likelihood that viewers will quickly skim only a portion of the many materials that could be provided in a web-based environment also suggests that, whatever the possibilities, few people will spend the time it usually takes to develop robust understandings of such complex material (Krug, 2000). As a consequence, the use of new technologies must go hand in hand with efforts to develop new genres and formats that can compress relevant materials into arrangements that viewers can grasp relatively quickly and easily. This process of compression is central to many scholarly disciplines, in which methods and genres have evolved to enable scholars to turn large amounts of data and information into forms that others can readily examine and understand.

Establishing some simple, commonly understood ways of storing and presenting teachers' expertise may make it much easier for teachers like Hutchinson, Capitelli, Cone, and their colleagues to represent previously unexamined aspects of their practice as well as to help wide audiences understand and build on what they have been doing. Many different forms and formats for representing teachers' expertise online are possible, including what Lee Shulman (1998) has called the "class anatomy." Like Hutchinson's website, a class anatomy website could focus on a single class, provide a series of videotapes that outline how the class unfolds, offer access to the materials used in the class, and share some evidence of the outcomes. Other website formats might include course evaluations that document course goals, course design, and outcomes; teacher inquiries that center around key questions and the curriculum materials, reflections, videotapes, and other data used to pursue them; and student portraits that focus on students' work and their learning and development over time.

New Educational Experiences: Closing the Gap Between Preparation and Practice

Developing web-based representations of teaching can also ground teacher education courses and professional development activities in the latest innovations and advances in teaching and learning in their own communities and from around the country. Renee Moore's website now gives teacher educators in Mississippi access to a host of materials that illustrate the practice of a Teacher of the Year award winner from their own state. Sarah Capitelli's website offers those working with elementary teachers in the San Francisco Bay Area a chance to look closely at evolving efforts to improve instruction in English in a bilingual classroom in a nearby community. Teachers and student teachers anywhere in the country can look at the work of Moore, Capitelli, and Hutchinson to examine key ideas and issues in teaching English across grades and contexts.

Nonetheless, turning these representations into a new source of ideas, knowledge, and resources in general and into productive educational experiences for teacher education students in particular is not an easy process (Lampert & Ball, 1998). As a result, we also need to document and learn from the efforts of teacher educators and others to create educational experiences that take advantage of the power of web-based representations of teaching.

Already, at Stanford University those studying to be teachers in Pamela Grossman and Krista Compton's class "Curriculum and Instruction in English" use Hutchinson's website as part of their assigned reading. Through a series of guiding questions and activities designed by Grossman and Compton (and inspired by the work of Lampert & Ball, 1998), the preservice teachers look at the videotapes of Hutchinson's classroom, study the strategies she uses, and apply them in the classrooms where they are student teaching. In addition to helping to build the preservice teachers' understanding of discussion-based teaching and providing them with concrete strategies and techniques they can try out right away, this experience also shows the aspiring teachers how much thought and planning goes into Hutchinson's teaching and the high levels of analysis and engagement that students can achieve when challenged and supported. Furthermore, these aspiring teachers can go on to share these techniques—and Hutchinson's website—with other colleagues they meet as they join the profession. In this manner, Hutchinson's extensive experience in the classroom and the specific strategies and techniques she has developed to work with a diverse group of learners become the foundation for the knowledge and practice of a new generation of teachers.

Ideally, in addition to drawing on the work and websites of nationally recognized teachers like Hutchinson, teacher educators could work with local professional development and reform organizations to identify teachers in their own local communities who are experiencing success with the students and in the schools where their aspiring teachers are most likely to work. These teachers could serve as a constant source for the development of websites that document the latest strategies and innovations of teachers who have been successful in working with all kinds of students, even under the most difficult conditions. For instance, as a part of the Apple Learning Interchange, the National Board for Professional Teaching Standards (NBPTS) is already experimenting with ways to turn the work samples, videotapes, and reflections produced by exemplary teachers as part of the NBPTS certification process into web-based resources for teacher education and professional development. Hundreds of other teachers who are involved in many of the most innovative reform efforts and are already inquiring into and documenting their teaching as part of their involvement in the National Writing Project and other professional development organizations could also contribute their expertise to online collections of teaching and learning in many different communities.

Teacher educators can also work with their recent graduates and alumni to develop their own websites that document their teaching. In the process, they can provide support and encouragement for their graduates to reflect on practice, foster new resources for their courses, and strengthen the relationships, mentorships, and support available to teachers both before and after they begin their careers. Making the teaching of their alumni public online can also help teacher educators see what strategies and ideas their graduates are applying in the classroom. In this manner, they can assess their programs and begin to build an online archive that provides a public demonstration of what their students learn in their teacher preparation courses and how they apply what they have learned in their own classrooms.

New Forums for the Constructive Examination of Teaching and Learning

The development of new educational experiences that take advantage of web-based representations of practice is just one step toward building the generative knowledge that can fuel improvements in teaching and learning. New representations of teaching and learning also demand new opportunities for viewers to share their interpretations, exchange perspectives, and inform one another's use of these materials.

Even in scientific disciplines that use traditional scientific methods and objective tests and experiments, results do not stand on their own; understanding what works—and why—depends on examination and interpretation. Similarly, in the arts, the interpretations of artists, critics, and others form an essential part of identifying "good" work. In both the arts and the sciences, the process of examination and interpretation is guided by a variety of peer review processes and vast bodies of commentary and critique. These discussions among communities of scholars, artists, and others help to develop the terms and language that can describe new phenomena, the criteria that can be used for assessment, and the broader knowledge and understanding that fuel public debate.

Like both scientific investigations and artistic works, teaching—with a practical imperative to have a positive impact on students and an ethical obligation to be consistent with community concerns and values—requires interpretation and the exchange of views and ideas about what constitutes effective and good practice. In contrast to the arts and sciences, however, there are few forums for the constructive exchange of views about those results or the thoughtful review of teaching more generally. As a consequence, in an era in which "high-quality teaching" has become a mantra for policymakers, there is no shared understanding of what high-quality teaching looks like or how to carry it out.

Given the wide reach of the Internet, an online collection of teaching and learning could be a foundation for a much broader and more constructive exchange of ideas among both experts and the wider public than has been possible in the past. One can imagine, for example, developing online journals that review representations of teaching and learning and offer different perspectives and viewpoints. Like art exhibitions, online forums could bring together different representations of teaching to highlight critical issues, describe new developments, and assess particular instructional strategies. Developing catalogs and commentaries to supplement these online exhibitions could build up the kind of critical discussions that help to advance work in architecture, visual and performing arts, and other disciplines.

In addition to developing more formal systems for review or expert commentary, engaging examples of teaching and learning and accompanying commentaries could be produced for and by many different audiences. Developing forums for the exchange and examination of web-based representations of practice in teacher education in particular could serve several crucial purposes. First, these forums could help to foster discussions of teaching in teacher education. Second, they could help to highlight the websites and issues that other teacher educators might find useful. Third, they could provide some examples and guidance that might help other teacher educators think about how to build on the work of K–12 teachers in their own practice.

Ideally, some of these other forums for examining representations of teaching could cut across the usual divides and facilitate the exploration of issues of teaching and learning across many different levels of education or even in international contexts. New forums for sharing web-based representations of practice and associated commentaries and critiques could also be designed to reach a wide range of public audiences. Many websites, such as www.GreatSchools.net, already offer parents and policymakers statistical information and test score data on schools around the country. Others provide opportunities for students to express their opinions about particular teachers, courses, and schools. But new websites, providing access to sophisticated online representations of teaching, links to expert commentaries, and opportunities for online discussions could provide a much more comprehensive view of the character and quality of the teaching taking place in many different schools and communities.

Just as professional and public discussions of new developments in the arts and sciences can create controversies and conflicts, online representations of teaching would likely engender some passionate debates. Differing beliefs and values about education and instruction; the political aspects of public schooling; and the personal investment of so many students, parents, and teachers can make discussions of teaching and learning particularly divisive. As a consequence, along with the effort to make teaching public on the Web, it would be essential to host discussions, both online and off, about the criteria used to decide which representations to highlight, how to ensure that commentaries are constructive, and how to provide adequate protection to teachers and students whose work might be made public and "critiqued." But such discussions and exchanges of views are precisely the ones that must occur to build a better understanding of the education that students receive now and the education they should receive in the future.

Toward the Future

New technologies can help teachers like Hutchinson and her colleagues to expand their influence and reach audiences that they could never reach either in person or through conventional publications, but this will entail thinking about the Internet as a new medium for the production of knowledge and the development of the scholarship of teaching and learning, not just a vehicle for disseminating lesson plans and course descriptions. In the process, in addition to developing new forms of representation, creating new educational experiences that use web-based representations, and establishing new forums for exchanging and critiquing those representations and the educational experiences that accompany them, other critical issues must also be addressed. Who will create these representations? What kinds of tools and resources will be developed to assist them? How will concerns about equity, issues of privacy, and questions about intellectual property be resolved? Furthermore, we have to come to terms with a "chicken or the egg" problem: it may remain difficult to categorize and organize web-based representations of practice without a common language to describe and highlight key aspects of teaching and learning in many different contexts, and it may remain hard to develop such a shared language without wider opportunities to see and examine the teaching and learning that goes on in many different classrooms.

Questions for Consideration

How can the Internet be used to develop and share teachers' knowledge?

What could web-based representations of teaching and learning look like? How might they be different from other forms of representation?

How could teacher education and professional development take advantage of web-based representations of teaching?

How could web-based representations be examined, critiqued, and used?

Notes

1. To view these examples and others, visit the Gallery of the Scholarship of Teaching and Learning developed at the Carnegie Foundation for the Advancement of Teaching (http://gallery .carnegiefoundation.org/). Several other organizations, including the Visible Knowledge Project at Georgetown University (http://crossroads.georgetown.edu/vkp/) and a series on "Images of Practice" at the National Center for Restructuring Education, Schools, and Teaching (NCREST) (www.tc.edu/ncrest/ website/images.htm), have also built on the examples and the technologies developed by the KML and the CASTL scholars to develop their own collections of web-based representations that focus on teaching and learning.

6

CONCLUSION

The preceding chapters illustrate both what it takes for teachers to make their teaching public and the ways in which they can have a positive impact on their peers and the wider profession when they do. The teachers described in this book learn as they teach. Moments of disequilibrium, concern, surprise, and unexpected success draw their attention to problems and issues that often linger in their minds. As they reflect on and sometimes study these issues on their own and with others, they begin to articulate what may be going on in their classrooms, and they start to develop the metaphors, language, and other representations that allow them to make their ideas public so that they can get feedback and have an influence on others. In the process, their efforts to examine their practice begin to open up the black box of the classroom and enable educators, researchers, policy-makers, and the general public to begin to imagine and understand what it takes to teach and learn in a wide variety of contexts.

The experiences of those involved in the CASTL program and the issues detailed throughout this book reaffirm that the current working conditions for teachers fail to provide adequate time and rewards for the careful examination of teaching and learning, but they also show how much can be done even under adverse conditions. As a consequence, the work of those who make their teaching public today provides only a glimpse of what might be possible if we truly had a system of education that recognized the complexity and sophistication of high-quality teaching and embraced the idea that teachers' expertise can be a critical resource in reshaping classroom practice and improving schools. The development of new supports and incentives can establish an infrastructure for learning from teaching that can enable many teachers to engage in much more powerful examinations of classroom practice than have been possible in the past. That infrastructure can begin to grow with even a few advances in existing school structures, including the creation of opportunities for both reflection *and* representation, the development of new avenues whereby teachers can present and publish their work, and the creation of new roles for knowledge brokers who can bridge the great divides among research, policy, preparation, and practice.

Reflection and Representation

The many existing initiatives designed to encourage teachers to reflect on their practice already provide opportunities for them to share their ideas with their colleagues. Often, however, these initiatives rely on conversations and personal interactions. Without adequate records of these conversations and without ways to summarize and capture the resulting ideas, the value of those conversations is limited by those who participate in them and by what those participants remember. By developing and recording categories, terms, labels, charts, narratives, and other representations, teachers can develop resources and artifacts that can advance their own learning and that they can share with others—in their own schools and beyond—who could not participate in those conversations. Simply keeping succinct notes on the key ideas emerging from conversations among teachers can help to keep those ideas in mind and make it possible for teachers and administrators to pursue and explore them over time.

Furthermore, unless these initiatives include opportunities for teachers to share those representations with superiors as well as peers, the positive influences that teachers can have on one another and the system as a whole may remain idiosyncratic and haphazard. Typical reporting tasks—including parent conferences, back-to-school nights, management team meetings, and board meetings—could be shifted from administrative and bureaucratic obligations into forums that give teachers opportunities to share the artifacts that emerge from their efforts to reflect on and represent their practice. Exhibitions and conferences in which teachers present annotated examples of their student work, display posters that illustrate classroom activities, or share the results of inquiries into key pedagogical questions can provide teachers with other forums in which to share their representations. Ideally, many of these initiatives would support the development and collection of the kinds of materials that could be presented on a website or as part of online collections that illustrate the kinds of teaching and learning going on in a particular school or community.

The current emphasis in many school districts on the collection of data on student performance and the use of data-based decision making could provide another set of opportunities for teachers to reflect on and represent their practice. Providing teachers with access to useful data on student performance, sophisticated assessments, and training in the use of powerful statistical tools may also go a long way toward establishing some of the supports that benefit researchers in other disciplines. However, the collection of data and other information should not be confused with learning and the generation of knowledge. Many approaches to data collection and data-based decision making in schools are intended primarily to gather information to fine-tune procedures and improve specific, narrow performance targets. Such efforts can make clear the need to improve and can help identify subjects, students, teachers, and schools for whom improvements may be needed, but they provide little of the substantive knowledge needed to make those improvements. In these approaches, there are few opportunities to generate or build on the kind of substantive knowledge that would enable school staff to develop the collective expertise needed to make significant and innovative changes in instructional practice and school structure; furthermore, attaching high stakes (including monetary rewards) to the outcomes of those data-collection efforts may provide a disincentive for teachers to take the kind of hard, critical look at their practice that the scholarship of teaching and the advancement of knowledge require.

New Avenues for Publication and Presentation

Although some professional development efforts are encouraging teachers to write about and present their work to their peers either in person or through online exchanges, these opportunities to document and represent teaching need to be connected to more formal and public occasions that can make teachers' work available for debate and discussion outside their own schools and networks. In other disciplines, formal and informal opportunities to share drafts of work, to make presentations, to produce handouts and graphics, and to submit works for review for publication and exhibition provide the deadlines, conversations, and feedback that motivate and support the development of new ideas. Such occasions also provide teachers like Capitelli, Boerst, Cone, Moore, Wolk, and Hutchinson with opportunities to shape their work to fit the demands of different audiences.

Some organizations—such as the National Writing Project, the National Council of Teachers of English, the National Council of Teachers of Mathematics, and the National Board for Professional Teaching Standards—already organize conferences and sponsor publications that give teachers these kinds of opportunities and incentives, and their efforts can serve as a foundation for developing the kind of pipeline of discussion groups, grants, presentations, and publications that is part of the infrastructure supporting the articulation of knowledge and development of ideas in other disciplines. The development of online publications and forums may also help to provide some of the incentives and feedback that can encourage teachers to make their teaching public.

Creating New Roles for Knowledge Brokers

Simply developing new representations and publishing or presenting ideas about teaching and learning does not necessarily mean that teachers will have any significant influence on researchers, policymakers, or practitioners more widely. However, the experiences of teachers like Capitelli, Boerst, Cone, Moore, Wolk, and Hutchinson suggest that their work can influence others when they—or the researchers and colleagues who work with them—go beyond their local schools and enter arenas and engage audiences with whom most other teachers rarely have contact. As knowledge brokers, these individuals can see, cite, and share the work of teachers and can take on the roles of translator, advocate, and amplifier to ensure that new ideas make their way to appropriate audiences and across the usual boundaries between teachers and the researchers, policymakers, and members of the general public responsible for the overall management and direction of teaching and learning.

At the moment, however, the work of knowledge brokers like these takes place as a sideline to their normal responsibilities as teachers or researchers. But one can imagine creating more formal roles, both inside K–12 districts and in institutions of higher education, with specific responsibilities for developing and sharing new knowledge on teaching and learning. These responsibilities could be made a part of initiatives to identify or reward "master" teachers or National Board candidates, efforts to develop coaches and mentors, or attempts to create new partnerships with research institutions. Whatever their character, these roles and responsibilities could be crafted to build on and build up the connections and networks through which teachers' ideas and influence can travel.

Summing Up

New opportunities to represent practice; to establish occasions for sharing those representations; to create the deadlines, audiences, conversations, and feedback that can reinforce and extend those exchanges; to connect those exchanges to formal opportunities to publish and present representations of teaching and learning for public consideration; and to foster the creation and influence of knowledge brokers—all these can help create an infrastructure for the examination of teaching and learning. These developments are crucial to fuel the creation and use of sophisticated representations of teaching and learning both online and off, and, in turn, increased opportunities to exchange artifacts and representations can help to establish the incentives and connections needed to build the infrastructure for examining teaching and learning more generally. Of course, many problematic issues remain to be worked out, including serious privacy concerns for teachers, students, and families, and questions of intellectual property—who owns and who might profit from the work of teachers and students. But as these issues are addressed, numerous benefits can emerge: new insights into the nature of teaching and learning; a visible history for the profession of teaching; an ever growing professional and public knowledge base; and closer connections among research, policy, preparation, and practice.

In the end, however, making teaching public may be most crucial for building a broader public understanding of what high-quality teaching and learning looks like and establishing a demand to make sure that all students receive it. When I recently went looking for a new home for my family outside of New York City, I was constantly reassured by real estate agents and community members that their schools were "good." As proof, they pointed to the high test scores in their schools. But none could tell me, with any detail, what went on in those schools. Only by going schoolhouse to schoolhouse to see fifteen different elementary schools in ten different communities could I get a sense of the kind of teaching and learning and the kinds of activities in which my children would be spending almost half their waking hours for thirteen years of their lives. But I can imagine a day when real estate agents refer prospective home-buyers to school websites where they can get access to the inquiries of teachers and see the kinds of classes and work their children will be involved in, not just the average test scores of their students. I can imagine college students and their parents who are trying to decide which courses to take and which colleges to attend surfing through examples of pedagogy and student work—not just skimming a course catalog, examining the average scores from student evaluations, or looking at the college rankings in US News and World Report.

As some schools and colleges make public the teaching that goes on inside them, students and their parents may well begin to expect and demand the opportunity to view the teaching that goes on in others. It is this kind of demand that requires changes in priorities. Those changes in priorities can in turn create changes in the ways in which time is spent. With new demands to see what is really going on in classrooms, K–12 teachers may be able to shift some of their time so they can document their teaching and reflect on students' learning. Similarly, this kind of demand can begin to influence the formal and informal reward systems and provide some new incentives for faculty to make their teaching public and for the public to give teaching the attention it deserves.

Creating this kind of demand for a professional culture that fosters the growth and development of every teacher may be what matters most in establishing the high-quality teaching force that so many are calling for today. Central to the development of that professional culture is the shift from viewing teachers as line workers who must be monitored and controlled to seeing them as scholars, able to investigate and learn from their activities, share their learning with their peers, and contribute to the advancement of the profession as a whole.

References

Ball, D. (1996). Teacher learning and the mathematics reforms: What we think we need to know and what we need to learn. *Phi Delta Kappan, 77*, 500–508.

Berliner, D. (1988). *The development of expertise in pedagogy*. Washington, DC: American Association of Colleges of Teacher Education.

Boerst, T. A. (2001). Problem solvers: Responses to the patterns in squares problems. *Teaching Children Mathematics, 8*(3), 169–172.

Boerst, T. A. (2003a). 24' × 30': Professing teacher knowledge beyond the classroom walls. *Teaching Children Mathematics, 9*(9), 499–501.

Boerst, T. A. (2003b). *The journey of ideas: The dynamics of learning and leadership*. Paper presented as part of a symposium at the American Educational Research Association, Chicago.

Boerst, T. A., & Schielack, J. F. (2003). Computational fluency. *Teaching Children Mathematics, 9*(6), 292.

Boyer, E. (1990). *Scholarship reconsidered*. Princeton, NJ: The Carnegie Foundation for the Advancement of Teaching.

Bransford, J., Brown, A., & Cocking, R. (Eds.). (2000). *How people learn*. Washington, DC: National Academy of Sciences.

Capitelli, S. (2000). *Bay Region IV final narrative*. Bay Region IV Inquiry Group at Mills College, Oakland, CA.

Carter, M. (2005). Helping African American males reach their academic potential. In T. Hatch, D. Ahmed, A. Lieberman, D. Faigenbaum, M. Eiler White, & D. Pointer Mace (Eds.), *Going public with our teaching: An anthology of practice*, (189–209). New York: Teachers College Press.

Cochran-Smith, M., & Lytle, S. (1993). *Inside/outside: Teacher research and knowledge*. New York: Teachers College Press.

Cochran-Smith, M., & Lytle, S. (1999). Relationships of knowledge and practice: Teacher learning in communities. *Review of Research in Education, 24*.

Cole, M., & Engestrom, Y. (1993). A cultural-historical approach to distributed cognition. In G. Salomon (Ed.), *Distributed cognitions: Psychological and educational considerations* (pp. 1-46). New York: Cambridge University Press.

Cone, J. (1992). Untracking AP English: Creating opportunity is not enough. *Phi Delta Kappan, 73*(9), 712–717.

Cone, J. (1993, Fall). The key to untracking: Learning to teach an untracked class. *College Board Review*, 20–27.

Cone, J. (1994). Appearing acts: Creating readers in a high school English class. *Harvard Educational Review, 64*(4), 450–473.

Cone, J. (2002, May 26). The gap is in our expectations. *Newsday*, p. 8.

Cone, J. (2003, May/June). The construction of low achievement: A study of one detracked senior English class. *Harvard Education Letter*.

Czarniawska, B., & Sevon, G. (1996). *Translating organizational change*. Berlin: Walter de Gruyter.

Dewey, J. (1904). The relation of theory to practice in education. In C. A. Murray (Ed.), *The relation of theory to practice in the education of teachers*. (Third Yearbook of the National Society for the Scientific Study of Education, Part I, pp. 9–30). Chicago: University of Chicago Press.

Eisner, E. (1998). *The enlightened eye: Qualitative inquiry and the enhancement of educational practice*. Upper Saddle River, NJ: Merrill.

Freedman, S. W., Simons, E. R., Kalnin, J. S., Casareno, A., & the M-Class Teams. (1999). *Inside city schools: Investigating literacy in multicultural classrooms*. New York: Teachers College Press.

Gardner, H. (1991). *The unschooled mind: How children think and how schools should teach*. New York: Basic Books.

Glassick, C. E., Huber, M. T., & Maeroff, G. I. (1997). *Scholarship assessed*. San Francisco: Jossey-Bass.

Greeno, J. (1997). On claims that answer the wrong questions. *Educational Researcher, 26*, 5–17.

Grossman, P., Smagorinsky, P., & Valencia, S. (1999). Appropriating tools for teaching English: A theoretical framework for research on learning to teach. *American Journal of Education, 108*, 1–29.

Hanson, M. (2001). Institutional theory and educational change. *Educational Administration Quarterly, 37*(5), 637–661.

Hatch, T. (1998). *Advancing the work of teachers, artists and scholars*. Paper presented at the Annual Conference of the American Educational Research Association, San Diego, CA.

Hatch, T. (2005). Introduction. In T. Hatch, D. Ahmed, A. Lieberman, D. Faigenbaum, M. Eiler White, & D. Pointer Mace (Eds.), *Going public with our teaching: An anthology of practice*, (1–13). New York: Teachers College Press.

Hatch, T., Bass, R., Iiyoshi, T., & Pointer Mace, D. (2004). Building knowledge for teaching and learning: The promise of the scholarship of teaching in a networked environment. *Change, 36*(5), 42–50.

Hiebert, J., Gallimore, R., & Stigler, J. (2002). A knowledge base for the teaching profession: What would it look like and how can we get one? *Educational Researcher, 31*(5), 3–15.

Hollingsworth, S., & Sockett, H. (1994). *Ninety-third yearbook of the National Society for the Study of Education, Part 1: Teacher research and educational reform.* Chicago: University of Chicago Press.

Huber, M. (1993). *Scholarship through history: A background paper for scholarship assessed.* Unpublished manuscript.

Hutchings, P., & Shulman, L. S. (1999). The scholarship of teaching: New elaborations, new developments. *Change,* 10–15.

Hutchinson, Y. D. (2005). *Thinking with text: An excerpt from "A friend of their minds."* In T. Hatch, D. Ahmed, A. Lieberman, D. Faigenbaum, M. Eiler White, & D. Pointer Mace (Eds.), *Going public with our teaching: An anthology of practice,* (181–186). New York: Teachers College Press.

Kingdon, J. W. (1984). *Agendas, alternatives, and public policies.* New York: Little, Brown.

Kozol, J. (1967). *Death at an early age: The destruction of the hearts and minds of Negro children in the Boston public schools.* Boston: Houghton-Mifflin.

Kronick, D. A. (1990). Peer review in 18th-century scientific journalism. *JAMA, 263*(10), 1321–1322.

Krug, S. (2000). *Don't make me think: A common-sense approach to web usability.* Berkeley, CA: New Riders Press.

Lampert, M. (1985). How do teachers manage to teach? *Harvard Educational Review, 55*(2), 178–194.

Lampert, M. (2001). *Teaching problems and the problems of teaching.* New Haven, CT: Yale University Press.

Lampert, M., & Ball, D. L. (1998). *Mathematics, teaching, and multimedia: Investigations of real practice.* New York: Teachers College Press.

Latour, B. (1986). Visualization and cognition: Thinking with eyes and hands. *Knowledge and Society, 6*(1), 1–40.

Lave, G., & Wenger, E. (1991). *Situated learning: Legitimate peripheral participation.* Cambridge: Cambridge University Press.

Little, J. W. (1990). The persistence of privacy: Autonomy and initiative in teachers' professional relations. *Teachers College Record, 91*(4), 509–536.

Little, J. W. (1999). Organizing schools for teacher learning. In L. Darling-Hammond & G. Sykes (Eds.), *Teaching as the learning profession* (pp. 233–262). San Francisco: Jossey-Bass.

Lortie, D. (1975). *Schoolteacher.* Chicago: University of Chicago Press.

March, J. G. (1999). Understanding how decisions happen in organizations. In J. G. March (Ed.), *In pursuit of organizational intelligence* (pp. 13–38). Malden: Blackwell Publishers.

Markus, H., & Zajonc, R. B. (1995). The cognitive perspective in social psychology. In G. Lindzey & E. Aronson (Eds.), *Handbook on social psychology* (3rd ed., Vol. 1, pp. 137–177). New York: Random House.

McDonald, J. P. (1992). *Teaching: making sense of an uncertain craft.* New York: Teachers College Press.

Moore, R. (2005). *Circles of influence: Use of dialogue circles in researching culturally engaged instruction*. In T. Hatch, D. Ahmed, A. Lieberman, D. Faigenbaum, M. Eiler White, & D. Pointer Mace (Eds.), *Going public with our teaching: An anthology of practice*, (77–91). New York: Teachers College Press.

Murnane, R., & Levy, F. (1996). *Teaching the new basic skills: Principles for educating children to thrive in a changing economy*. New York: Free Press.

Nonaka, I. (1994). A dynamic theory of knowledge creation. *Organization Science, 5*, 14–37.

Pointer Mace, D., Hatch, T., & Iiyoshi, T. (in press). In R. Goldman, R. Pea, B. Barron, & S. Derry (Eds.), *Video research in the learning sciences*. Mahwah, NJ: Erlbaum.

Rose, M. (1996). *Possible lives: The promise of public education in America*. New York: Penguin.

Rosenholtz, S. J. (1989). *Teachers' workplace: the social organization of schools*. White Plains, NY: Longman.

Roth, W.-M., & McGinn, M. (1998). Inscriptions: Toward a theory of representing as social practice. *Review of Educational Research, 68*(1), 35-59.

Schön, D. (1983). *The reflective practitioner*. New York: Basic Books.

Seely Brown, J., & Duguid, P. (2002). *The social life of information*. Boston: Harvard Business School Press.

Sfard, A. (1998). On two metaphors for learning and the danger of choosing just one. *Educational Researcher, 27*(2), 4–13.

Shirley, D. (1997). *Community organizing for urban school reform*. Austin: University of Texas Press.

Shulman, L. S. (1986). Paradigms and research programs in the study of teaching. In M. C. Wittrock (Ed.), *Handbook of research on teaching*. New York: MacMillan.

Shulman, L. S. (1987). Knowledge and teaching: Foundations of the new reform. *Harvard Educational Review, 57*(1), 1–22.

Shulman, L. S. (1993). Teaching as community property, *Change, 25*(6), 6–7.

Shulman, L. S. (1998). Course anatomy: The dissection and analysis of knowledge through teaching. In P. Hutchings (Ed.), *The course portfolio: How faculty can examine their teaching to advance practice and improve student learning* (pp. 5–12). Washington, DC: American Association for Higher Education.

Solomon, G., & Perkins, D. (1998). Individual and social aspects of learning. *Review of Research in Education, 23*, 1–24.

Spiro, R. J., Feltovich, P. J., & Coulson, R. L. (1992). Cognitive flexibility, constructivism, and hypertext: Random access instruction for advanced knowledge acquisition in ill-structured domains. In T. M. Duffy & D. H. Jonassen (Eds.), *Constructivism and the technology of instruction: A conversation* (pp. 57-75). Mahway, NJ: Erlbaum.

Star, S. L., & Griesemer, J. M. (1989). Institutional ecology, "translations," and boundary objects: Amateurs and professionals in Berkeley's Museum of

Vertebrate Zoology, 1907–1939. In M. Biagioli (Ed.), *The science studies reader* (pp. 505–524). New York: Routledge.

Stenhouse, L. (1983). The relevance of practice to theory. *Theory into Practice, 22*(3), 211–215.

Stenhouse, L. (1988). Artistry and teaching: The teacher as focus of research and development. *Journal of Curriculum and Supervision, 4*(1), 43–51.

Tyack, D. (1974). *The one best system: A history of American urban education.* Cambridge, MA: Harvard University Press.

Wenger, E. (1998). *Communities of practice.* Cambridge: Cambridge University Press.

Wideen, M., Mayer-Smith, J., & Moon, B. (1998). A critical analysis of the research on learning to teach: Making the case for an ecological perspective. *Review of Educational Research, 68*(2), 130–178.

Wiggins, G., & McTighe, J. (1998). *Understanding by design.* Alexandria, VA: Association for Supervision and Curriculum Development.

Wolk, E. (1997). *Progressive education in conservative times.* Paper presented at the American Educational Research Conference, Chicago.

Wolk, E. (1998). *Diversifying the research team: The inclusion of students and community members.* Paper presented at the American Educational Research Conference, San Diego, CA.

Wolk, E. (2004). *Getting the green light: The transformative power of participatory action-research with students as researchers.* Paper presented at the American Educational Research Conference, San Diego, CA.

Index